*Context and Culture in Language
Teaching and Learning*

Languages for Intercultural Communication and Education

Editors: Michael Byram, *University of Durham, UK*
and Alison Phipps, *University of Glasgow, UK*

The overall aim of this series is to publish books which will ultimately inform learning and teaching, but whose primary focus is on the analysis of intercultural relationships, whether in textual form or in people's experience. There will also be books which deal directly with pedagogy, with the relationships between language learning and cultural learning, between processes inside the classroom and beyond. They will all have in common a concern with the relationship between language and culture, and the development of intercultural communicative competence.

Other Books in the Series
Audible Difference: Speaking English as a Second Language and Social Identity in Schools
    Jennifer Miller
Critical Citizens for an Intercultural World: Foreign Language Education as Cultural Politics
    Manuela Guilherme
Developing Intercultural Competence in Practice
    Michael Byram, Adam Nichols and David Stevens (eds)
How Different Are We? Spoken Discourse in Intercultural Communication
    Helen Fitzgerald
Intercultural Experience and Education
    Geof Alred, Michael Byram and Mike Fleming (eds)

Other Books of Interest
Foreign Language and Culture Learning from a Dialogic Perspective
    Carol Morgan and Albane Cain
The Good Language Learner
    N. Naiman, M. Fröhlich, H.H. Stern and A. Todesco
Language, Culture and Communication in Contemporary Europe
    Charlotte Hoffman (ed.)
Language Learners as Ethnographers
    Celia Roberts, Michael Byram, Ana Barro, Shirley Jordan and Brian Street
Language Teachers, Politics and Cultures
    Michael Byram and Karen Risager
Motivating Language Learners
    Gary N. Chambers
New Perspectives on Teaching and Learning Modern Languages
    Simon Green (ed.)
Teaching and Assessing Intercultural Communicative Competence
    Michael Byram

Please contact us for the latest book information:
Multilingual Matters , Frankfurt Lodge, Clevedon Hall,
Victoria Road, Clevedon, BS21 7HH, England
http://www.multilingual-matters.com

**LANGUAGES FOR INTERCULTURAL COMMUNICATION
AND EDUCATION 6**
Series Editors: Michael Byram and Alison Phipps

Context and Culture
in Language Teaching
and Learning

Edited by

Michael Byram and Peter Grundy

MULTILINGUAL MATTERS LTD
Clevedon • Buffalo • Toronto • Sydney

17 MAY 2010

Library of Congress Cataloging in Publication Data
Context and Culture in Language Teaching and Learning/Edited by Michael Byram and
Peter Grundy.
Languages for Intercultural Communication and Education: 6
Includes bibliographical references.
1. Language and languages–Study and teaching–Social aspects.
I. Byram, Michael. II. Grundy, Peter. III. Series.
P53.8 .C68 2002
418'.0071–dc21   2002015981

British Library Cataloguing in Publication Data
A catalogue entry for this book is available from the British Library.

ISBN 1-85359-657-4 (hbk)

Multilingual Matters Ltd
UK: Frankfurt Lodge, Clevedon Hall, Victoria Road, Clevedon BS21 7HH.
USA: UTP, 2250 Military Road, Tonawanda, NY 14150, USA.
Canada: UTP, 5201 Dufferin Street, North York, Ontario M3H 5T8, Canada.
Australia: Footprint Books, PO Box 418, Church Point, NSW 2103, Australia.

Printed and bound in Great Britain by Short Run Press Ltd.

Contents

Introduction: Context and Culture in Language Teaching and Learning

Mike Byram
University of Durham, School of Education, Durham DH1 1TA, UK

Peter Grundy
University of Durham, Department of Linguistics, Durham DH1 1TA, UK

Context and Culture in Language Teaching and Learning is a topic that has developed in many directions and with considerable vigour in the last 10 to 15 years. The origins lie partly within theory and practice of language teaching, and partly in response to the recognition of the social and political significance of language teaching. The two are not unconnected. The advances made in terms of defining the 'content' of language teaching, the emphasis on speech acts, functions of language and the analysis of needs, for example, have led to a greater awareness of learners as social actors in specific relationships with the language they are learning, relationships which are determined by the sociopolitical and geopolitical circumstances in which they live. Simultaneously, methodologists have developed a more differentiated view of learners as human beings with feelings and identities which have to be taken into account by those who wish to help them to learn.

'Context' is thus as complex a concept as 'culture', the latter being notoriously difficult to define. 'Culture' in language teaching and learning is usually defined pragmatically as a/the culture associated with a language being learnt. Of course this begs many questions. It is to address some of these questions and others related to 'context' that a conference with the title *Context and Culture in Language Teaching and Learning* was organised at the University of Durham in June 2001. This was one of a series linking the universities of Durham, Besançon and Bremen as part of a partnership between the three universities to pursue common research interests for students and staff. The partnership is however not closed and other universities may join us, just as contributors from other universities were welcomed at the conference.

All the articles except one began as contributions to the conference. The exception is the first article, by Claire Kramsch, which was written at the invitation of the editors. We saw that articles fell into two broad categories: those by Holme, Holtzer, and Fäcke are reports of empirical studies of learners; Halbach, Decke-Cornill, Wandel and Breidbach focus on teachers and teaching, their purposes and methods.

Taking a single instance of learner talk, Holme shows how culture is encoded in the everyday conceptual metaphors speakers take for granted. He describes the way these encodings differ across languages as 'semantic relativism' and argues that language teachers need to be aware of this phenomenon. Only then can they fully understand their learners' interlanguage and help their learners to recognise the internal structure of the prototypical categories of the language they are learning.

Whereas Holme's focus is on the way lexical items reflect culture, Fäcke's project shows how the reading of literature is determined by the learners' response as social actors with specific cultural identities. Thus each learner individualises the learning experience and comes to very different conclusions about the meaning of a common text.

The third empirical study of learners is Holtzer's account of the way that cultural identity is mediated in intercultural telephone conversations used as learning devices. As learners encounter otherness and the identity of 'native' speakers and culture members, both learner and native member set out to assist the other in the process of cultural understanding. Most notably, it is the native members who make the most use of communication strategies as a means of enabling non-native members to acquire the linguistic representations of the target culture.

The fourth paper in this collection is Halbach's empirical study of trainee teachers, and focuses in particular on the difficulties that 'other' methodology in the form of reflection poses for those unused to such a learning culture. Halbach suggests procedures that can make imported methodology appear less 'other', but ultimately concludes that 'other' methodology needs also to be adapted to some degree to the local context and culture.

Decke-Cornill also presents an empirical study of teachers and change, but with the focus on teachers already working in schools. She identifies two types of response to the possibility of teaching English as a lingua franca, where there is a break of the traditional assumption that a language is associated with one or more specific cultures. Those with academic qualifications in the study of English teaching in selective schools are more reluctant to accept the notion of teaching a lingua franca than those teaching in comprehensive schools often with few or no academic qualifications. Although taken from the German context, the issues raised are significant for most teachers of English, and for those who train and educate them.

Wandel's article also deals with the teaching of English and the cultures with which it is traditionally associated, and demonstrates an alternative approach where India is the focus. One of the points he makes however is that the choice of India introduces more clearly the need for attention to the affective response of learners to other cultures, a need which has to be anticipated in textbooks.

The debate on English is taken a step further by Breidbach's contribution which considers the position of English in the gradual political and social integration of Europe. There is a tension between the wish to preserve European linguistic and cultural diversity and the practical needs of people to interact with each other within the newly emergent social and political structures. Breidbach thus places the debate on language teaching firmly in the wider context and offers a model of curriculum design which would meet the need for both diversity and ease of communication through the widespread use of English.

The authors of all these articles differ in the degree of explicitness about their research methods and theories, depending in part on the nature of their article; but one article from the conference, by Wendt, expressly addresses the issues of theory formation for foreign language teaching by taking a broad view and suggesting the directions in which the discipline should move. This therefore seemed the obvious concluding article and we decided to invite Claire Kramsch, well known for her empirical as well as theoretical work, to reflect on how she in practice does her research. We are grateful that she responded to this with enthusiasm, allowing her readers behind the scenes of empirical research and theory development, and this gave us an excellent starting point for our collection.

Correspondence

Any correspondence should be directed to Professor M. Byram, School of Education, University of Durham, Durham, DT1 1TA, UK (m.s.byram@durham.ac.uk).

From Practice to Theory and Back Again

Claire Kramsch
Department of German, University of California, Berkeley CA 94720, USA

A research project may begin in a 'telling moment' in the language classroom. This article describes the phases of a research project as the author moves from classroom to library, from empirical data to theoretical framework and back again. The methodology includes a comparative dimension through the collection of data from learners in three countries and demonstrates the development of insights from these three sources to gain deeper understanding of learners in the classroom from which the research questions originated. The research process thus becomes the beginning of new processes and plans for the classroom.

In the Classroom

This Wednesday morning, in my 11 o'clock third semester German class, I am discussing with my 15 undergraduate students the short story by Yüksel Pazarkaya *Deutsche Kastanien* that they have read the night before. The story is about a 6-year-old boy, Ender, born and raised in Germany of Turkish parents. Ender is snubbed one day in the schoolyard by his best friend Stefan, who doesn't want to play with him anymore because, he says, Ender 'is not German but an *Ausländer* [a foreigner].' Ender runs back home and asks his mother 'Who am I? Turkish or German?' The mother doesn't dare tell him the truth. The father answers: 'You are Turkish my son, but you were born in Germany' and tries to comfort him with the promise that he will talk to Stefan.

As a warm-up exercise, I have brainstormed students' responses to the questions: 'Why do people leave their country, what problems do they encounter in a foreign country?' The students are quick to offer all kinds of reasons and problems, for the situation is familiar to many of them. They have no difficulty expressing themselves in German: 'People look for opportunities, for a job, but they have no money, no friends, no family, they don't know the language, they can't find a job, there are many prejudices, cultural differences ...'. To prepare the class for the topic of the story, I then engage them in the following exchange in German:

CK: What do you associate with the word *Ausländer* [foreigner]?

Ss: (silence)

S1:   different?

CK: yes, people who are different, foreign (I write both words *anders, fremd* on the board). In America, who is an *Ausländer*?

Ss: (long silence)

S1:   (hesitantly) In Germany *Ausländer* are all the people who don't look like Germans.

      (long silence)

S2:   Here in America ... people can look different, many have an accent, bad English ...

S3:   Or no English!

S4: (half to himself) Are there any *Ausländer* here in America?

The students' silence and S4's question puzzle me. Why are the students suddenly so reluctant to speak? And why does S4 seem to believe that there are no foreigners in the United States? I switch topic and turn to the story proper. The class becomes lively again. I make myself a note to remember this incident and to further explore the matter.

The telling moment

Most of my research is triggered by such 'telling moments' in the classroom – my misunderstanding of a student's utterance, an unusual silence, a student's unexpected reaction, a grammatical or lexical mistake that doesn't make sense to me. Or sometimes it is just that the class that I prepared so well totally bombed and I don't know why. On the way back home, I replay the scene in my head, examining all its facets. I tell about it to my colleagues and friends: Has that ever happened to them? What do they think? What went wrong? I talk to some students I trust: what is their take on the event? Slowly I piece together a range of possible interpretations. Some tell me that Americans, unlike the Germans, don't care about who is a foreigner or a native, provided one lives in the country. People that are here illegally are a matter for the police, not for private citizens. Some tell me that it is not politically correct to talk about foreigners, or even to identify anyone as a 'foreigner', that it is almost a slur, which is why foreign students in the US are called 'international' students. Others tell me that American students probably don't understand why the boy in the story is not a German citizen, if he was born and raised in Germany. They probably think that Ender is a first-generation German, not a Turk. Yet others suggest that my questions were too vague, so the students didn't know how to answer.

Building up to a research project

So if the term *Ausländer* has different connotations for a German and an American, then perhaps the American students resonate quite differently to the story than I do. I decide to find out how they understand the story by having them write in class, in their own words, a 4–5 sentence summary of what the story is about. I collect the 15 summaries and, that night, I compare them to one another. To my amazement, not only are the summaries all very different, but the students' point of view comes across sometimes very visibly in the way the students have constructed their summaries. Take, for example, the following:

> 1. Diese Geschichte ist uber einer jugend. Er heißt Ender. Und er hat eine Probleme weil, sein Freund ihm sagte daß er kein Deutscher ist. Und alles wo Ender geht, die Menschen sagt zu ihm daß er kein Deutscher ist. Er ist ein Ausländer von Türkei.

> (This story is about a youth. He is called Ender. And he has a problem because his friend told him that he is not a German. And wherever Ender goes, people say to him that he is not a German. He is a foreigner from Turkey.)

In this summary, notwithstanding the occasional case and gender errors, the combined effect of the lack of conjunctions between the sentences, the repetition of 'daß er kein Deutscher ist', and the lapidary last sentence, renders well the sense of sadness this student intends to convey. But the direct borrowing, into German, of the American phrase 'he has a problem' (*er hat eine Probleme*) inserts into this summary the voice of a society where problems are seen to lie with the individual rather than with society.

In the next summary, the evaluative voice of the student comes out clearly in the last sentence (italics are mine):

> 2. Es gibt ein Türke Kind, das Ender heißt, das in Deutschland wohnt. Er ist im Deutschland geboren, und er spricht Deutsch am besten. Er geht zu eine Deutsche Schule, und seine Freunden sind Deutsche. Aber, die Deutsche Kinder sind ihm böse und sie sagen das Ender keine Deutsche ist, weil seine Eltern Türke sind. *Das wird schwerer, wenn er älter wird.*

> (There is a Turkish child, who is called Ender, who lives in Germany. He was born in Germany, and he speaks German best. He goes to a German school, and his friends are German. But the German children are nasty to him and they say that Ender is not a German, because his parents are Turkish. *It will be more difficult when he is older.*)

This last sentence voices the point of a view of an author who knows something about discrimination and has no illusions about its eradication. We hear such indignant authorial voices also in the following three passages where again I put the student's evaluation in italics:

> 3. Seiner Vater kann die Fragen nicht gut antworten. Die Geschichte fragt die Frage, daß wenn ein 'Ausländer' in Deutschland geboren ist, er ist Beider ein Deutscher und ein Türker. *Wie kann dieser Mann was etwas zu tun wissen? Er ist in die Mitte von zwei unfreundliche Seiten.*

> (His father cannot answer the questions well. The story asks the question that if a 'foreigner' is born in Germany, he is both a German and a Turk. *How can this man know what to do? He is in the middle of two unfriendly sides.*)

> 4. Er wünschte zu wissen – wer bin ich? *Dieses Problem kommt oft wenn man ein Ausländer ist. Es ist die Frage 'Was ist der Unterschied zwischen uns? Aber es gibt keinen Unterschied in realität, außerdem daß der superficiel ist. Die Kastanien sind ein Symbol. Es bedeutet das wir unsere Unterschiede machen.*

> (He wants to know - who am I? *This problem often often comes when one is a foreigner. It is a question 'What is the difference between us? But there is no difference in reality apart from that it is superficial. The chestnuts are a symbol. It means that we make our differences.*)

> 5. Die Jungen sagte, 'Sie sind Deutsche Kastanien! Du bist kein Deutscher!' *Aber, die Kastanien und Ender sind beide jetzt Deutch!*

> (The boys say 'They are German chestnuts! You are not a German!' *But the chestnuts and Ender are both German!*)

I can see that these summaries are not merely a miniversion of the same original story, but narrative constructions in their own right. Some are longer than others, some read like a police report, others like a personal commentary, yet others like a precis. Some include an evaluation or a moral, others extract the philosophical truth of the story as in the following simple summary:

> 6. Es ist über was ist und nicht ist deutsch. Deutsch Vorurteil sagt, daß man nicht anders sein kann. Also, wer ist Ender? Wie kann man deutsch werden?
>
> (It is about what is and is not German. German prejudice says, that one cannot be different. So, who is Ender? How can one become German?)

while others remain close to the facts. Through these summaries, I start hearing the voices of the individual students: puzzled, empathetic, outraged, academically savvy. I can see how much of themselves and of their view of the world they have projected into these summaries. Also, I discover that there are different ways of writing summaries: some are general impersonal statements about the theme of the story (as in summary 6), others tell the facts in their original sequence but in shorter form, others contain extensive evaluations of the events in the story (as in summary 4). The students have been taught differently how to write summaries, depending on which school they went to.

I am, of course, particularly curious to find out how these summaries express the plight of *Ausländer* in Germany. I discover that the students either avoided the topic 'foreigner' altogether and described the story as a story of discrimination against a child from 'an ethnic minority', or they tried to coin words impossible in German like 'first generation German' or 'Turco-German' that reflect their American understanding of the situation. I am starting to see that the silence I experienced in class was more than a linguistic problem; it was a cultural problem.

Reviewing the Research Literature

Where should I turn to for a better understanding of what's going on? I start making myself a list of what I have found and that I need to read up on:

- First, I need to inform myself about the recent immigration laws in Germany. Why is Ender not German? When can a child born in Germany of foreign parents become a citizen? What are the facts?
- The German word *Ausländer* evidently evokes mental representations that are different from those evoked in American English by the word *foreigner*. For an American, a schoolboy like Ender evokes: ethnic minority, Anglo-Americans vs. recent immigrants. For a German, the story evokes: xenophobia, Germans vs. foreigners. Each of these terms evokes a different frame, script, or schema of expectation. I need to read up on connotations, associations, frames and schema theory (Cook, 1994; Goffman, 1974; Tannen, 1979).
- Language doesn't only represent or refer to social reality (here, the original text the students had in common), it constructs social reality, e.g. the very term *Ausländer* evidently constructed the difficulty we had in discussing *foreigners* in the US. I need to read up on the relationship of language and social structure (Halliday, 1978), discursive roles (Goffman, 1981), social constructionism (Shotter, 1993) and to re-visit the literature about the rela-

tionship of language, thought and culture also called linguistic relativity (Gumperz & Levinson, 1996).

- Writers construct not only reality, but a discoursal self through their discursive choices. I need to read up on the discursive features of narratives (Fowler, 1986; Short, 1996) and on the relation of discourse and identity in writing (Ivanic, 1998).
- Even in such short summaries, there is often a distinct evaluative component that expresses an authorial point of view. I need to read up on evaluation in narrative (Hunston & Thompson, 2000; Hymes, 1996; Labov, 1972).
- Finally, texts are not written free of generic constraints. The genre that I imposed on the students, the summary, seems to have its own conventions and expectations that constrained what students could and could not write. I need to read up on genre as social practice (Swales, 1990).

Thus, as I explore the various facets of the incident, I start looking to how applied linguistics research and theory might help me phrase some of my original puzzled queries into research questions. As I delve into the theory, other aspects of the practice emerge which I had not noticed or for which I had no name. For example, as I read up on writing and identity, Ivanic's term 'discoursal self' comes in handy for my purposes. What the students were constructing through their written summaries was, of course, not a permanent social identity, but a kind of textual identity (Kramsch & Lam, 1999) or discoursal self (Ivanic, 1998) that expresses how they position themselves *vis-à-vis* the story, i.e. their subject-position. In the same manner as the author of the story makes his authorial or discoursal self clear through his rhetorical style and the way he tells the story, so do my students' discoursal selves become apparent in the way they exercise authorial control and point of view through their choice of what they say, what they don't say, in their 4–5 sentences.

What they don't say … in order to say other things. As I write this sentence in my notebook, I am reminded of an article I had read by A.L. Becker on the six dimensions of difference in the way people 'language experience' (Becker, 1985). He makes the point that one has to give up saying many things in order to say other things, and that each one of us places the silences differently. He calls this the 'silential' dimension of difference. Other dimensions he mentions are: the referential (we refer to a reality within or outside of language), the structural (we shape the grammar), the generic (we shape the genre), the medial (we shape the medium), the interpersonal (we shape a relation with our listener/reader). How did each of my students shape reality in that way? What did each of them *not* mention, that was mentioned by others? Perhaps I could find in this insight a way of organising class activities so that students can compare their summaries for what each says or doesn't say, and for how they structure their discourse. I jot down in my notebook: 'Have all the students write their summaries on the blackboard for subsequent general discussion of their dimensions of difference?'

As I read I find new ways of phrasing my observations in the terms used by researchers. I now understand Germans' views of *Ausländer* not just as a different way of naming immigrants, but as a whole different 'mental structure of expectation' (Tannen, 1979) or 'conceptual schema' (Cook, 1994) that includes different scripts of behaviour, e.g. the distinction between *Inland* and *Ausland*, the notion of not belonging, or not being a citizen, the connotation of temporary status associated with being an outsider or *Ausländer*. Americans, I hypothesise, don't have this category, because they expect anyone who lives in this country to 'belong' here, to be an insider, irrespective of whether they are actually citizens or (legal or illegal) aliens. In fact, the word 'alien', a legal term that would correspond to *Ausländer*, seems to be hardly used in everyday parlance to refer to someone living in the US. But wait ... Is this really so? Am I not espousing a White middle-class Anglo-American bias? Most American students do understand discrimination based on race and ethnicity, especially if they belong to an ethnic minority group, even though this discrimination is not necessarily phrased in terms of national identity and of *Deutsche* vs. *Ausländer* as in Germany. As I read through the literature, trying to make sense of my 'telling moment', I write down my thoughts in my notebook. Writing things down, sometimes in English, sometimes in German, helps me link the thoughts to the language in which they are most easily expressed and to the different worldviews they represent.

Research Questions

By now I have dipped into the readings in the five areas I jotted down. They give me ideas as to how to frame my research questions:

(1) How do students construct the foreign cultural reality through the foreign language? To what extent are learners' written productions constrained by culturally determined discourse genres?
(2) What stylistic resources do learners draw upon to appropriate for themselves someone else's text? How do their stylistic choices differ from those of native speakers and other learners?
(3) What discoursal self do the students construct in the process, i.e. how do they construct themselves as authors?
(4) What implications do these findings have for the way we teach foreign languages?

Methodology

At this point, I consider the initial summary exercise in my classroom as a pilot study, and decide to replicate it in other classes, with a total number of 62 American undergraduate students of a third semester course taught in three different classes. I add a series of semi-structured interviews with two dozen focal students, chosen so as to provide a wide range of summary styles and contents. On a voluntary basis, they agree to reflect on their summary and tell me why they wrote it the way they did and what they thought about the story.

I further want to compare my American students' summaries with those of students from a different national background. So I contact a French teacher of German, that I know, at a lycée in Nantes and ask her to do the same exercise with her 21 senior students, thus ensuring that they are roughly the same age (16–20) as the Americans, and, perhaps, at an equivalent level of proficiency, considering that they have had only two years of German as a second foreign language. I am also very interested to see how native speakers of German would summarise that same story, at the same age level, in various schools in Germany. I write to a teacher I know from a Realschule in Lübeck, who agrees to do the exercise with her 24 senior students. She refers me to two secondary school teachers, one from a Gymnasium in Passau in West Germany, one from a high school in Leipzig, from the former East Germany, who agree to do the same with their 24 and 14 students, respectively. This hopefully will allow me to highlight the differences in the way American, French and German youngsters from different social classes and geographical appartenances, construct themselves and the characters in the story. Given the long distance contact I establish with the teachers at those schools, I cannot control the number of students nor really the way the assignment is presented. But I am not trying here to conduct a watertight experiment with tightly controlled variables. Mine will be a descriptive study, in which I establish categories of analysis for use in a pedagogy of language awareness and self-reflection for the authorial empowerment of the students.

Findings

The summaries of 'Deutsche Kastanien' by students from France and Germany confirm my hypothesis that the genre *summary* (French *résumé*, German *Zusammenfassung*) is a culturally marked genre. Representative samples of each cultural group are reproduced below. They show that the summaries by the American and French learners of German (cf. summary 7) remain close to the human interest story and its factual aspects, whereas the summaries by the German native speakers (summaries 8, 9 and 10) focus on the larger problem, of which Ender's story is only an illustration.

> 7. Sample summary from 1ère Lycée Nantes
> Es handelt sich um einen Text über zwei Kinder Stephan und Ender. Stephan sagt ihm, daß es für einen Fremder verboten ist, deutsche Kastanien anzuziehen, weil Ender Türke ist. Ender wird traurig, daß sein bester Freund mit ihm noch nie durch dieser Grund nicht spielen will. Doch kommen seine Eltern aus Türkei aber er ist in Deutschland geboren. Sein Vater sagt ihm, daß er mit Stefan sprechen wird, damit er netter mit Ender zu sein versuchen wird.
>
> (It is about a text about two children Stephan and Ender. Stephan says to him that it is forbidden for a foreigner to pick German chestnuts, because Ender is a Turk. Ender becomes sad that his best friend does not want to play with him any more for this reason. [Although] his parents come from Turkey, he was born in Germany. His father tells him that he will talk to Stephan, so that he will try to be nicer to Ender.)
>
> 8. Sample summary from Class 10b Gymnasium Passau
> In der Kurzgeschichte 'Deutsche Kastanien' von Yüksel Parzakaya wird der Junge Ender mit Ausländerhaß konfrontiert. Als sein bester Freund Stefan nicht mehr mit ihm in der Pause Fangen spielen will, ist Ender traurig, betroffen. Aber als ihn dann auch noch am Nachmittag zwei Kinder aus dem Grund, er sei kein Deutscher, einschüchtern, macht ihn das nachdenklich. Doch auf seine Identitätsfragen können ihm selbst seine türkischen Eltern keine Antwort geben, da Ender eigentlich in Deutschland geboren, aufgezogen und zur Schule geht, daher ein Deutscher wäre.

(In the short story 'German Chestnuts' by Yuksel Parzakaya, the boy Ender is confronted by hatred of foreigners. When his best friend Stephan does not want to play catch with him in the break, Ender is sad, hurt. But when furthermore in the afternoon two children bully him because he is not a German, he begins to think. However even his Turkish parents cannot give him an answer to his identity question, since Ender in fact was born, brought up and goes to school in Germany, and therefore should be a German.)

9. Sample summary from Class 9a Realschule Lübeck

Problemstellung: Das Problem besteht darin, daß ein türkischer Junge aufgrund rassistischer Äußerungen nicht weiß, wo er hingehört

Inhaltsangabe: Ender darf bei einem Spiel nicht mitspielen, weil er Türke ist. Andere Kinder hindern ihn daran, Kastanien zu sammeln aufgrund derselben Tatsache. Weil er nun unsicher ist, fragt er seine Mutter, um Klarheit zu schaffen. Diese weicht ihm aus. Also spricht er mit seinem Vater, der ihm den Sachverhalt erklärt und die gewesenenen Zustände (ohne Rassismus) wieder herstellen will.

Eigene Meinung: Meine Meinung dazu ist, daß das Problem Ausländerfeindlichkeit zu groß ist, als das es von einem normalen Menschen durch reden bewältigt werden könnte.

Problem formulation: The problem lies in the fact that a Turkish boy does not know where he belongs because of racist remarks.

Summary of content: Ender is not allowed to take part in a game because he is a Turk. Children stop him from collecting chestnuts for the same reason. Because he is now unsure, he asks his mother to explain. She avoids answering him. So he speaks to his father, who explains the facts to him and intends to re-establish the past situation (without racism).

Own opinion: My opinion is that the problem of hatred of foreigners is too big for it to be handled by one person talking.)

10. Sample summary from the Humboldt-Schule, Leipzig

Es geht um einen kleinen Jungen, dessen Eltern aus der Türkei stammen, er selbst aber in Deutschland geboren wurde. Vom Gesetz her ist der Junge also Türke, er fühlt sich aber als Deutscher und versteht deshalb nicht, weshalb er von anderen Kindern als Ausländer bezeichnet wird. Seine Eltern können oder wollen ihm darauf auch keine richtige Antwort geben. Der Junge steht zwischen zwei Kulturen und weiß nicht, zu welcher er eigentlich gehört. Die Geschichte spricht die Ausländerfreindlichkeit in Deutschland an und die Probleme der Integration von 'Ausländern' an.

(It is about a small boy whose parents are from Turkey, but who himself was born in Germany. Legally then the boy is a Turk, but he feels German and therefore does not understand why he is called a foreigner by other children. His parents can't or won't give him a proper answer to this. The boy stands between two cultures and does not know to which he really belongs. The story is about enmity towards foreigners in Germany and the problem of the integration of 'foreigners'.)

Of course, differences in linguistic proficiency might account for much of the difference seen in the summaries above. It is clear that the French and American authors avoid or do not have the skill to build the complex and embedded sentences that their German counterparts build. But from a stylistic perspective, there is variety among students from various schools in Germany as there is between the French and the American summaries. The French summaries remain generally more faithful to the definition of a 'summary' given by the French Department of Education:

> The summary follows the line of the narrative. It gives a condensed, but faithful, version of the text, in the same order as the text … It reformulates the discourse of the original text without taking any distance to it … It highlights the articulations of thought. In a reduced form, it reconstructs the rhetorical thrust of the text. (Kramsch, 1996, my translation)

The German summary requires the reproduction of the 'meaningful elements' (*sinntragende Elemente*) of a text. From sample summary 9, it is clear that students in the Realschule in Lübeck have learned to give a tripartite structure to their summaries: *Problemstellung* (enunciation of the problem), *Inhaltsangabe* (summary of the contents), *Eigene Meinung* or *Persönliche Stellungnahme* (personal opinion or evaluation), which the Leipzig students have not.

The American summaries show a great deal of variety; they do not all adhere to the definition of the genre as given in Memering and O'Hare's *Guide to Effective Composition*:

> A summary is the condensation of the information in a longer text. To write a summary:
>
> - get the main idea;
> - use your own words;
> - follow the organization of the original
> - record only the information contained in the text, and nothing else. Keep your opinions to yourself. Do not add commentary, interpretation, or anything else not in the original. (Kramsch, 1996: 178)

Contrary to the injunctions above, most of the American students in my data do not hesitate to express opinions and to evaluate the story (see summaries 3–5).

Besides discovering the cultural influence of genre on the macrolevel of the students' written summaries, I find that the students make use of a wide variety of stylistic resources and are quite conscious of the choices they made both on the macrolevel of text organisation and on the microlevel of sentence structure, grammar and vocabulary.

On the macrolevel, they have decided how much text space to devote to which aspect of the story, how much of their 4–5 sentences they would devote to evaluation, how much to description; they have chosen to focus on one theme rather than another, for example, Ender's problem, or the parents' helplessness, or the general political situation; and they have decided on what not to mention from the original story.

On the microlevel, they have decided how to start their summary. For example, some first sentences focused on Ender as a child ('Es gibt ein Kind, das heißt Ender' *There is a child who is called Ender*), some on Ender as a Turk in Germany ('Deutsche Kastanien' geht um einen Jungen, der Ender heißt, der ein Türker-Deutscher ist' *'German Chestnuts' is about a boy who is called Ender, who is a Turkish-German*), others on Ender's identity crisis ('In der Geschichte 'Deutsche Kastanien' der Junge der Ender heißt hat eine Problem – eine Identitätskrise' *In the story 'German Chestnuts' the boy who is called Ender has a problem - an identity crisis*), or on the friendship problem ('Eine Kind hatte Schwierigkeit mit seine Freunde' *A child had difficulties with his friends*), or on the larger issues ('Die Geschichte handelt von der Konfrontation eines türkischen Jungen mit Ausländerhaß' *The story is about the confrontation of a Turkish boy with hatred of foreigners* or 'Die Geschichte beschreibt die Situation eines jungen fast Ausländer, der in Deutschland wohnt' *The story describes the situation of a young person almost a foreigner who lives in Germany*).

Beyond this point of departure, I can see that some decided to write their summaries in the present tense, others in the past tense, others with a mixture of tenses. Some used spatiotemporal markers such as 'one day' or 'in the school-yard', others left the summary in an indefinite time and place. Some, especially the American students, used short main clauses separated by periods. Others used to varying degrees coordinated and/or subordinated clauses, separated by semi-colons, commas and periods, with adverbs and conjunctions. Summaries varied in the syntactic and lexical choices of their authors, even though one might say that, in the case of the learners of German, choice was often determined by availability and access, i.e. degree of proficiency.

However, I find that despite their limited proficiency in the language, the American and the French learners of German make effective use of stylistic resources like prosodic rhythm, lexical repetition and parallelism, that give their summaries cohesion and coherence (e.g. summaries 1 and 2). I can thus synthesise for myself an answer to my research question 2 (see Table 1).

Table 1 Stylistic resources used by native and non-native authors

Macrolevel	Microlevel
Genre	Point of departure
Theme	Sequencing tenses
General organisation	Spatiotemporal markers
Text time vs. story time	Syntactic choices
Evaluation vs. description	Lexical choices
Silences	Cohesive devices

On the macro and microlevel of the text, stylistic choices affect the ideas that are expressed and the stance the author takes *vis-à-vis* the reader. Following Halliday (1978), one could say that the textual function of language reinforces the ideational and the interpersonal functions. For example, as we saw above, writing 'Ender hat eine Probleme' positions the author *vis-à-vis* a certain ideological 'way with words' that has currency in the student's context. Similarly, the exclamation 'aber, die Kastanien und Ender sind beide jetzt Deutch!' is addressed to a reader who is assumed to understand the American point of view on this story, thus positioning both author and reader within a common cultural horizon.

In my interviews with the American focal students, I gain further insights into the motivation for these students' authorial choices. Let us take as an example my interview with the author of summary 6, a white, male student from Los Angeles, a few weeks after the exercise:

S: … kinda nice to read it again. Those are definitely, I think, the things that still stick out for me the most … Personally, I find it a rather German story … It looks like the children, who are saying you are not German, seem to have a sense of what it means to be German.

CK: Are you saying that here it is more difficult to say who's American?

S: Yes and no. Because I think … by default you'd end up saying everyone is American. Because there are no lines that you can draw. It would be hard to define what American culture is. Yes … you're American, you live here.

CK: What does it mean to be American?

S: … hm … so much of … what it means to be American is … to distance yourself from those kinds of notions. I think … um … where … being American isn't as important as … the specific niche you fill, or … how your life works out individually.

CK: So, even asking the question … marks you as non-American?

S: Right.

I realise that a Chinese-American or a Mexican-American would be likely to hold quite a different discourse from this white, male student from Los Angeles, and that, in the same manner that the German students from Lübeck, Passau and Leipzig have very different ways of understanding and summarising the same story, I must be cautious not to take 'Americans' as representative of one mono-lithic culture (for details see Kramsch, 1996)

Back in the Classroom

As I pull together the strands of my observations and analyses, and go back into my classroom, I summarise some of the thoughts I want to hold on to and explore further at a later date.

I wanted to find out how my students understand the problem of *Ausländer* in Germany, how they use the linguistic and stylistic resources of the German language to express a cultural reality that is foreign to them, and what kind of discoursal selves they construct in the process. I found that, despite their obvious linguistic limitations, these learners were eminently able to shape the various dimensions of difference within native and non-native cultural frames; they were able to account for their stylistic choices, even if they had to admit that choice was often reduced by a limited access to grammar and vocabulary. Their summaries resignified the original story into a story that made sense to them and in which they could evaluate the events from the perspective of their own worldview. Many of the American summaries reflected American attitudes and reactions to the situation of Turkish children in German schools. Although most of them didn't grasp the political and legal aspects of discrimination against foreigners in Germany, they all resonated to the human aspect of the story, based on their own experience.

From my reading, I understood that German 3 students were not just reproducing the contents of a story in 4–5 sentences. By having to choose what not to say, and what to say and how, they constructed a version of social reality that corresponded to their understanding of the social order and of their place in it that often differed both from the original version and from that of their fellow students. It was often tempting to categorise their reactions to the story in terms of 'American' and 'German' culture and I fell into that linguistic relativity trap myself, for example when I suggested that the phrase 'Ender has a problem' might reflect an individualistic ideology prevalent in my students' environment. It is certainly a fact that the English language, as currently used in the United States, makes it easy to use this phrase in all kinds of contexts, thus opening the door for such a reading. But one may not infer stable, permanent attitudes and beliefs from a one-time linguistic behaviour.

What does such an informal ethnographic study, based on a telling moment in the flow of classroom discourse, suggest for the way I teach German? I can draw several direct implications of my findings for my own practice.

- Rather than merely measuring up my students against native speakers' 'correct' or 'appropriate' use of linguistic structures, I decide to pay more attention to the creative ways in which they make use of the full range of semiotic (linguistic, discursive, pragmatic, aesthetic) resources of the language to express whatever meaning they wish to express. Such a pedagogy would focus on the student, not as deficient non-native speaker, but as authorial voice and as creator of meaning (see Kramsch 1993, 1995, 1996, 2000).
- To validate my students' authorial voices, I have to enable them to justify their choices, even if they reconstruct after the fact an authorial intention of which they were only dimly aware at the time of writing. The purpose is less to know what they 'intended' to write, than how they interpret what they have written.
- A general class discussion comparing and contrasting authorial voices can enhance students' discoursal selves without laying bare students' autobiographical selves (see Ivanic, 1998). Asking students to write their summaries on the chalkboard, for example, for general discussion, can help them appreciate the unique way they use language when they compare it to others (e.g. Kramsch, 2000).
- Teaching students how to analyse their own texts gives them a critical metalanguage to appreciate their own and other writers' semiotic resources (see Hunston & Thompson, 2000; Short, 1996).

The research approach I have described here looks, of course, much more linear and straightforward than what took place in reality. The researcher/teacher goes from the data to the theory to the data, and back to the classroom where the data came from, in a constant shuttle between the micro and the macro picture, trying to make sense of the details without losing a sense of the whole. In this process, there always comes a moment in one's reading, one's data collection or one's analyses where doubts start to appear: Was this really what was happening in my German 3 class on that Wednesday morning? Am I not giving undue importance to what was after all a fleeting incident? Is stylistic analysis really necessary?

The truth is, research does not only explain existing moments, it has a way of revealing other potentially intriguing moments, that might be even more relevant or worthy of research than the initial one. Thus, I initially wanted to understand why my students constructed the word *Ausländer* differently from me, and ended up examining how they constructed the whole story and themselves in the process. I wondered why the students did not understand Ender's problems of identity, and became interested in the authorial identity of my students, and in the role language played in the construction of both. I also came to realise that focusing originally on the students who spoke up in class that day, I was ignoring those who remained silent, such as the Japanese-American woman in the back of the class who confessed to me during the interview that she would never dare voice any opinion on 'foreigners' in the US for fear of antagonising the Anglos in the class.As such, this exploration opened up for me 'avenues for future research', as they say. From the rhetoric of my students' summaries, I became interested in their discoursal selves and in the ways I could facilitate the development of their authorial voices.

Ultimately, back in the classroom, this excursion into theory has broadened my outlook on my practice. I now listen to my students within a different frame. I hear their silences and imagine what they chose not to say. I notice their choice of words, I detect their American cultural assumptions behind their German phrases, I am much more cautious about saying 'Germans do this, Germans do that', when talking about so-called native speakers, for I remember the summaries by the students in Leipzig that were so different from their Passau or Lübeck counterparts. But most of all, I am now intent on validating my students' choices, by asking them explicitly to interpret them and find a rationale for them. I hope thereby to help them find pride in their use of the foreign language and to make them aware of their power to construct, in that language, worlds different from their own.

Correspondence

Any correspondence should be directed to Dr Claire Kramsch, Department of German, University of California, Berkeley, CA 94720, USA (ckramsch@socrates.berkeley.edu).

References

Becker, A.L. (1985) Language in particular: A lecture. In D. Tannen (ed.) *Linguistics in Context: Connecting Observation and Understanding. Advances in Discourse Processes (Vol. XXIX) R.O. Freedle (ed.).* Norwood, NJ: Ablex.
Cook, G. (1994) *Discourse and Literature.* Oxford: Oxford University Press.
Fowler, R. (1986) *Linguistic Criticism.* Oxford: Oxford University Press.
Goffman, E. (1974) *Frame Analysis.* New York: Harper and Row.
Goffman, E. (1981) *Forms of Talk.* Cambridge, MA: Harvard University Press.
Gumperz, J.J. and Levinson, S. (eds) (1996) *Rethinking Linguistic Relativity.* Cambridge: Cambridge University Press.

Halliday, M.A.K. (1978) *Language as Social Semiotic. The Social Interpretation of Language and Meaning*. London: Arnold.

Hunston, S. and Thompson, G. (eds) (2000) *Evaluation in Text. Authorial Stance and the Construction of Discourse*. Oxford: Oxford University Press.

Hymes, D. (1996) Ethnopoetics and sociolinguistics: The stories by African-American children. In *Ethnography, Linguistics, Narrative Inequality. Toward an Understanding of Voice*. London: Taylor and Francis.

Ivanic, R. (1998) *Writing and Identity. The Discoursal Construction of Identity in Academic Writing*. Amsterdam: John Benjamins.

Kramsch, C. (1993) *Context and Culture in Language Teaching*. Oxford: Oxford University Press.

Kramsch, C. (1995) Rhetorical models of understanding. In T. Miller (ed.) *Functional Approaches to Written Text: Classroom Applications*. Special issue of *TESOL France The Journal* 2, 61–78.

Kramsch, C. (1996) Stylistic choice and cultural awareness. In L. Bredella and W. Delanoy (eds) *Challenges of Literary Texts in the Foreign Language Classroom* (pp. 162–84). Tubingen: Gunther Narr.

Kramsch, C. (2000) Social discursive constructions of self in L2 learning. In J. Lantolf (ed.) *Sociocultural Theory and Second Language Learning* (pp. 133–54). Oxford: Oxford University Press.

Kramsch, C and Lam, E. (1999) Textual identities: The importance of being non-native. In G. Braine (ed.) *Non-Native Educators in English Language Teaching* (pp. 57–72). Mahwah, NJ: Lawrence Erlbaum.

Labov, W. (1972) The transformation of experience in narrative. In *Language in the Inner City: Studies in Black English Vernacular*. Philadelphia: University of Pennsylvania Press.

Short, M. (1996) *Exploring the Language of Poems, Plays and Prose*. London: Longman.

Shotter, J. (1993) *Conversational Realities. Constructing Life Through Language*. London: Sage.

Swales, J. (1990) *Genre Analysis*. Cambridge, MA: Cambridge University Press.

Tannen, D. (1979) What's in a frame? Surface evidence for underlying expectations. In R. Freedle (ed.) *New Directions in Discourse Processing*. Norwood, NJ: Ablex.

Carrying a Baby *in* the Back: Teaching with an Awareness of the Cultural Construction of Language

Randal Holme
University of Durham, Department of Linguistics, Durham DH1 1TA, UK

In the communicative era, language teachers tend to focus on 'culture' according to a combination of five views: the communicative view, the classical curriculum view, the instrumental or culture-free-language view, the deconstructionist view, and the competence view. The first three views treat cultural content as marginal or even irrelevant to successful language learning. The last two views treat language and culture as being acquired in dynamic interaction, with one being essential to the full understanding of the other. They assume that language and culture actually shape and interpenetrate each other in accordance with Whorf's (1956) relativistic studies of language and meaning. This assumption was once questionable but Whorf's conclusion is now supported by the cognitivist interest in how the conceptual structures that underlie abstract and, hence, grammatical meaning may be culturally constructed (e.g. Gibbs, 1994; Heine, 1997; Lakoff, 1987; Lakoff & Johnson, 1999).

Five Views of Culture

The introduction of 'culture' into the language curriculum can be rationalised according to five principles. These principles are by no means mutually exclusive and may often work in combination. Nonetheless, they vary greatly in their perception of how central language teaching is to culture. I will call the first the communicative view, the second the classical-curriculum view, the third the culture-free-language view, the fourth the deconstructionist view, and the fifth the competence view.

The *communicative view* is derived from the communicative approach with its stress on giving the student language that can be put to quick use in a specific context. This approach detracts from any belief that a language may be inherently valuable. Culture, when introduced, is a source of what Dudley-Evans and St John (1998: 11) call 'carrier content' for the language points from which it is held to be separate. For example, if a teacher introduced a video on recent race riots in the UK, the instrumental nature of much communicative teaching would insist that the video's primary purpose would not be to acquaint students with the tensions that prevail in Britain's multi-culture. The video's purpose would be to enhance discussion skills, or more specifically, to acquaint students with a discourse peculiar to the situation that is being shown – the register of protest, perhaps, whatever that would be.

Second is the *classical-curriculum view*, where the interest of languages is secondary to how they function as access routes to the alien and, in some sense, enlightening modes of thought which their host communities are held to have engendered. Accordingly, the culture to which the language gives access can also enhance the intellectual value of the language. This provided a rationale for the learning of Ancient Languages, whose construction was held to inculcate their students with principles of logical thought, perhaps because their grammar was somehow associated with the rationalist philosophical tradition to which they gave birth.

I will call the third the *instrumental or culture-free-language view*. This view could proceed from a common concern in respect of the hidden political and cultural agenda of a language. Phillipson's (1992) thesis argues that a dominant language such as English is owned by the socioeconomic centre of global power that comprises the BANA (British, Australasian and North American) countries. The language emanates out from this 'centre' towards 'the periphery' as a mechanism of cultural and epistemological impoverishment for those located there (Phillipson, 1992: 52). Implicit in this argument is the view that a language will become a mechanism of cultural transmission, promoting the values of its host-culture against those of the regions to which it is exported. Thus, the widespread adoption of English-medium education in the Gulf could be perceived as making those countries into perpetual consumers not just of the language of the BANA states but of the knowledge and value systems implicit in it. The obvious counter would be to declare linguistic independence by developing Arabic as a medium for modern scientific education.

However, although it is difficult to imagine that the language advisers of the Gulf might share the post-Marxist core of Phillipson's thesis, they do possess a strong awareness of the dangers of cultural contamination implicit in the learning of a dominant international language. They have responded in two quite different ways, according to the age and objectives of the learners. The first response is to contextualise the target language in the students' own region and culture. The implicit argument is that a culture does not exist in the core of language but is its movable background and can be changed like the scenery of a play. The second response is to perceive scientific, financial or technological knowledge as value-free. Language should therefore be learnt in order to afford access to communities that share knowledge or socioeconomic function. At face value, English for Science or Medicine may proffer a discourse neutered of the subversive cultural influence of the general English course-book with its overt propagation of Western teenage values. Rightly or wrongly, such a belief makes an implicit rejection of a central deconstructionist tenet by ascribing to a traditional objectivism that holds Science to be free of cultural values and language to be without any implicit cultural representation. I will now examine this deconstructionist view.

The fourth *deconstructionist view* embraces many quite different strands of thought. It might draw first upon on the critical literacy perspectives and critical discourse analysis of Fairclough (1989), Hodge and Kress (1993), or Maybin (1994), where the cultural construction of text means that the language student may be manipulated by that text's implicit messages. Language learning should entail an understanding of such meanings.

First, a view of language as a social construction might carry teachers back towards the SFL (Systemic Functional Linguistic) analysis of language by which it was partly spawned. The Hallidayan concept of language as a social semiotic perceives a language's structure as reflecting the communicative needs of a given social context. A language which is fashioned around the representation of meanings in society has been interpreted by scholars such as Fairclough (1989) as a language of socially constructed meanings. This interpretation moves language from its more neutral representation of a social context towards the perpetuation of the social order and the value systems implicit in its forms of use.

I can exemplify what these approaches might mean in classroom by referring briefly to a feature of language that the SFL tradition has identified as grammatical metaphor. A grammatical metaphor is 'the expression of a meaning through a lexico-grammatical form which originally evolved to express a different kind of meaning' (Thompson, 1996). Central to the scientific use of grammatical metaphor is the nominalisation common in the expression of cause and effect relationships, as in a phrase such as 'glass crack growth' (Halliday, 1993: 79). The metaphor occurs because this phrase refers to a process 'growing' which should congruently or naturally be expressed as a verb but which is here represented by a noun phrase. According to Halliday (1993: 71), grammatical metaphor complicates the task of interpreting English scientific discourse because it is not congruent with the natural expression of things as nouns and actions as verbs by which language is characterised. Although it complicated the interpretation of language, grammatical metaphor is thought central to the expression of science because it allows a writer to set up a cause and effect relationship between processes rather than between the objects through which those processes are mediated. Thus, 'heating increases glass crack growth' foregrounds a relationship between two processes 'heating' and 'growth' by treating them as if they were things. By contrast, the congruent sentence, 'if you heat the glass it will crack more quickly', places a reduced emphasis upon the relationship between the processes. However, writers also use such devices in order to assume a mantel of spurious scientific authority. An expression such as 'the revolution triggered the inevitable reaction', for example, constructs history as a clash of events in a manner that denies the power of agency to its prime actors, namely human individuals. Deconstructing the use of such nominalisations might provide students both with an enhanced critical understanding of certain types of text and of the mechanisms through which they can themselves participate in the construction of a prestigious form of discourse. The Hallidayan analysis of language can therefore become useful as a tool of classroom deconstruction that will also help students grapple with forms central to the expression of scientific meanings.

I call the fifth classroom approach to language and culture the *competence view* (e.g. Byram, 1989; Byram & Fleming, 1998; Byram & Risager, 1999). This view contends that the knowledge of a language's culture is thought essential to a full understanding of a language's nuances of meaning. Knowledge of a culture presupposes a competence which is essential to the grasp of language's true meaning. Thus, learning a language should be completed by a sustained and ethnographically structured encounter with the language's culture (Roberts *et al.*, 2001). An ethnographic approach to culture is different from the critical discourse approaches just described. There is no sense of a culture as a reified, exotic object that propagates itself by infusing language with a conspiracy of implicit meanings. A sense of culture evolves out of a sense of difference between ethnographers and the practices that they document. This can be examined through the area of literacy. Street (1996) has argued consistently that literacy cannot be perceived as a singular cultural product encapsulating a single core value system. It is a series of social practices that surround the use and creation of written language. Arguably, this view is extensible to language itself, since literacy is at root a use of language. Therefore we can discover the relationship between language and culture in the different language-based practices of different groups in different societies. Yet, a language, by the fact of its being intelligible to its users, constructs itself as a singular entity whose code will be unlocked by the acquisition of a singular core competence. As said, linguistic practices are, in their diversity, antithetical to the concept of a monolithic culture. However, because a language has a singular nature, it is likely, over time, to become the single collecting ground for the products of the diverse cultural practices in which it is involved. And among these practices, one should number how a language's community of users will conceptualise their reality.

Therefore, although the deconstructionist and the competence view both start from very different positions, each reaches the same broad assertion that language is to some extent a cultural construction. For the language teacher, such an assertion raises two core questions: (1) Is there linguistic evidence for how culture affects the nature of language? (2) Should the nature of this effect alter their approach to classroom teaching?

In this paper, I briefly examine the first question by summarising how evidence from the discipline of cognitive linguistics is overturning older, universalist assumptions about the relationship of language to culture. I next look at one instance of how my answer to the first question can affect classroom approaches to the teaching of meaning in a language – in this case English. I will do this by recounting a pedagogical episode in the role of participant observer and then by analysing the same and proposing a possible response.

The Influence of Culture upon Language

According to Whorf (1956), language affected how a culture conceptualised reality. Different languages evolved different ways of seeing. Yet, when Chomsky (e.g. 1965) focused linguistic inquiry upon a universalist quest for the structures that underlie all language, Whorf's relativist position on culture and language became unfashionable. The culturally shaped differences among languages appeared trivial when compared to their common, underlying features.

Semantic primitives

Universalist views of language proposed a reductionist search for the common components of meaning. For example, Wierzbicka (1980) identified a set of 13 semantic primes or primitives that were employed in all languages and which were incapable of further subdivision. Though the list was later expanded, these primitives were initially, 'I, you, someone, something, world, this, want, not want, think of, say, imagine, be part of, become'.

Yet, Wierzbicka's recent work (1986, 1997) attests to how one should be wary of the assumption that there is a simple dichotomy between those who would emphasise the universal features of language and those who would perceive it as a construct that reflects cultural relativism. While not denying the plausibility of her earlier reductionism, Wierzbicka (1986, 1997) has focused on meanings that are less elementary than the universal primes from which all meaning has emerged. A given primitive will be divided by language into meanings that may vary from one language to another in response to a cultural effect. She attests, for example, that the Australian English concept of mateship, exemplifies a division of the semantic domain of friendship which is sufficiently different between languages for it to mitigate against its easy translation. Mateship cannot be properly understood outside the context of a history of convict settlement (Wierzbicka, 1997). Yet one should stress that this type of analysis does not overturn a hierarchy that is founded upon universal primitives. Rather, it reveals how the universal components of meaning are partitioned differently according to the way in which culture shapes language.

Wierzbicka is not putting forward a psychological theory of meaning construction. Yet, Wierzbicka's earlier interest in the reduction of culturally divided meanings to their common primitives does operate a concept of category construction if only as a mechanism with which to postulate a system that can explain the nature of meaning. Individual phenomena, mangoes and strawberries for example, must first be reduced through their common properties to fruit, and fruit reduced to the common property of something. There is an assumption that categories are made possible by ignoring the individual differences between phenomena and settling on attributes that are common to them. This reduction of different phenomena to a core of common attributes suggests a move towards increasing abstraction. It is paradoxical, that if, in the end, we reduced these fruits to one of Wierzbicka's primitives, something, we would have attained the highest degree of abstraction possible.

Cognitivist views of meaning move in the exactly opposite direction (e.g. Gibbs, 1994; Johnson, 1987; Lakoff, 1987; Lakoff & Johnson, 1999). On the evidence of a diachronic study of language, the meaning of a mango is not seen as generated from the concept of something; rather, our idea of something is extracted from the physical experience of phenomena in the world, the individual fruits.

Cultural realisation of universals

Wierzbicka suggests a balance between the universal primitives of meaning construction and their culturally affected realisation. This balance can offer the teacher the sense that, although such culturally determined differences are finely drawn, they nonetheless exist. She can therefore foster an awareness as to how language students may have to cope with slight differences in the way their L1 and their TL divide up the same fundamental semantic territory. Yet she does not offer a sense that this culturally induced reapportionment of the same semantic territory will be the source of a vast gulf of misunderstanding that should justify the inclusion of a cultural component into a language curriculum. Furthermore, the process of meaning construction is not postulated as a psycholinguistic theory that can identify mechanisms of control over the process of meaning generation which will help students to produce the culturally appropriate form. Cognitive linguistics, however, may help to furnish teachers with something more substantive.

As said, a corner-stone of the cognitive analysis of language is that it roots not in universal abstraction but in the experience of ourselves as physical beings and through this our interaction with the world as a physical entity. This is not to propose that our cognition, or the part of it devoted to visual processing, is initially cluttered by thousands of instances of a given phenomenon and then extracts common visual or functional features in order reconstruct them as a category. The proposition is about the nature of meaning construction as beginning in the experience of ourselves as embodied minds and in the impact of the world upon that state of being (Johnson, 1987). I can illustrate this better with a very different category to 'fruit' – that of 'direction'.

The difficulty with 'direction' is that it is almost entirely abstract, in the sense of having no physical exemplars from which it could have been deduced. Therefore, in order to be established as a category, direction must always be represented as something other than itself. In language, prepositions express the subordinate categories of direction. Some examples of these in English are 'ahead', and 'back/behind'. Interestingly, these prepositions, show how our sense of ourselves as physical beings has been used to form a subcategory. Heine (1997) describes how prepositions often evolve from the parts of the body that best characterise the orientation they describe. This can be seen clearly in the examples I have just given. 'Ahead' comes from the fact that our forward facing visual system gives us a sense of walking 'head forwards'. 'Behind' and 'Back' both derive from the parts of our anatomy we cannot normally see and thus refer to a direction that we cannot track visually.

Two fundamental conclusions can be drawn. The first is that meaning is not generated out of abstract universals. Abstraction is achieved through a metaphor of physical experience. Hundreds of other examples have been found in order to show that abstract experience is almost entirely constructed out of such metaphors of embodied experience (Lakoff & Johnson, 1999). The second point is that if any semantic primitives are to be found, it is in the way in which we schematise our early physical experience of ourselves and the world. To give another example, an infant hauling itself upright for the first time will generally show an expression of immense satisfaction and happiness. The infant will equate happiness with being upright. They will thereafter create a schema equating upwardness with happiness. Grady (1997) has called these schematised experiences, primary metaphors. Upward and downward states will themselves propose a resource, called image schemas, to describe other abstract sensations and emotions (Johnson, 1987). The image schemas are used by other conceptual metaphors such as up is more, up is good, down is bad, down is hurt, etc.

At first sight, it might now appear that we have simply shifted back to an argument in favour of universal meanings. The meanings do not root in abstractions, but in the universals of physical experience as these are experienced by a common, human anatomy. However, this is far from being the case. Physical experience is not common to humanity everywhere, only some attributes of it are. We grow up experiencing different segments of reality with groups of individuals whose natures vary and who engage in radically different types of activity. Some of our early experiences are universals of existence. However, our perception of these will sometimes be through the filter of different cultures. The fact of growing up in a different culture may also alter the nature of the experiences themselves. These differences mean that we may conceptualise even universal experience through different metaphors (Gibbs, 1994; Lakoff, 1987). I can illustrate this with a quite extreme and very radical example.

Time

Time finds universal expression in language. However, like direction, time, as an abstraction, cannot be envisaged except through something else. Interestingly, the conceptualisation of time is closely bound up with spatial direction. Perhaps the most common or basic conceptualisation of time is as space (Lakoff & Johnson, 1980). Applying this analysis, an English conceptualisation of time is as an object or person moving in space, as a resource with a spatial existence, or as space itself. For example, the phrase, 'time is passing fast', refers to an object moving in space, and 'we have a long way to go' to time as the space we move in, while, 'I've used up my hour', treats time as a resource that we consume.

Lakoff and Johnson (1999) put forward the notion of an 'event structure hierarchy'. According to this hierarchy, a fundamental metaphor such as 'time is space' means that the vehicle of the metaphor, space, will lend its structure to the 'topic' time. Therefore, if an event occurs in space, it will unfold within the parameters furnished by the structure of space. Because 'time is space', events that occur in time will also be subject to the parameters of that structure. For example, we can say that 'space permits directional movement that is forwards or backwards', therefore 'time permits directional movement that is forwards or backwards' because time is space. At this point in the hierarchy, it would seem likely that we are still dealing with universals. An event structure hierarchy ensures that all languages probably discuss changes in time as

> forward or backward movement. The metaphor, 'time is space', and the event structure hierarchy evolving from it are crucial to a device as fundamental as the analogue clock. Yet, the event structure hierarchy does not determine which time is in front and which time is behind.

The speakers of most languages have adopted a common principle in the conceptualisation of time. They appear to have abstracted the arc travelled by the sun into a line. They have situated themselves on that line with dawn at their back and the sunset ahead. The sun's movement begins at one point and ends at another. The movement of the sun is a primordial representation of time. Time therefore left one point and moved towards another. Time is both the sun and the space over which the sun moves. Most carry this concept within them, conceiving of the future as spatially in front and the past as spatially behind. Thus, 'we go back into the past' or we decide that 'we are going to do something in the future', as if the action 'do' were a place towards which we were moving. The event structure hierarchy determines that 'time' must have a backward point and a forward point relative to ourselves as creatures located in this linear space. It does not decree that the backward point should be the past in the way a solar metaphor might suggest. Interestingly, some languages construct the future behind and the past in front. There is another logic to this that is unrelated to factors such as the movement of the sun. The future is unknown and what is behind cannot be easily seen, while the past is known, because it has been accomplished.

One such language is an Amerindian language, Ayamaran, in Chile (Núñez *et al.*, 1997). What we are seeing here is a cultural effect in respect of how a language conceptualises time. The language transmits a cultural value in its core structure (Lakoff & Johnson, 1999: 141). Few language learners have to bridge gaps that are quite this radical. However, this example makes a clear point about how a culture achieves a given affect. Such examples have led some cognitive linguists to revisit Whorfian relativism, but with a different conclusion. The conclusion is that it is not the patterns implicit in language which impose themselves on a culture's modes of thought but the metaphors through which a culture conceptualises reality that impose themselves upon language (Gibbs, 1994: 438–45).

Conceptual Metaphors

I can also give a quite different illustration of how culture affects language through conceptual metaphor. In this example, the effect of culture occurs at a lower, less prominent, place within an event structure hierarchy. The effect is also far less central to an understanding of a particular language. However, such effects are common and reveal how cultural preoccupations fashion meaning. The effect does not impact upon a language's grammatical core, but upon its idiom. Idiom is overtly metaphorical. Idiom also occurs with varying degrees of prominence. It can be studied as encapsulating different forms of conceptual metaphor (Gibbs, 1992).

In English, a 'red herring' signifies a diversion in a conversation or monologue from what should be the main topic. It can also be an active attempt to divert a speaker from their chosen subject. The idiom derives from the practice where convicts used rotten herrings to divert bloodhounds from a scent (Goatly, 1997: 32). A central conceptual metaphor is that states are treated as locations (Lakoff & Johnson, 1999: 180–183). By the same token, objectives are landmarks that we try to reach. Landmarks can move or become a quarry that we have actively to hunt. It is probably common for language to perceive a goal as an animal or human we have to track down. By the event structure hierarchy, a failure to achieve a goal is a failure to hunt down one's prey. Correspondingly, devices that distract from the attainment of a goal are devices that divert a pursuit.

Hunting metaphors are, doubtless, common to many cultures. Arguably, they are even primal and remain central to the conceptualisations of people who never chase people or animals. Pursuing convicts with dogs represents an interpretation of hunting that is more specialised. The use of rotten fish to distract dogs is very specific. It is therefore at this less general level that we start to see a strong cultural effect on metaphor formation, resulting in the idiom, 'I smell a red herring'.

The examples I have given are historical. They show how a language bears the imprint of the many cultures that have made use of as it has developed over time. Through these analogies, a language transmits the perceptions of generations of users, fashioning current thoughts according to conceptualisations that were made generations before. Yet conceptual metaphors are not merely fossils that we learn to use with a language, but with which we have no active engagement. They continue to play a part in how we conceptualise new meanings or extend the expression of old (e.g. Gibbs, 1994; Lakoff & Johnson, 1999). This can be illustrated with a straightforward example from French.

As discussed, a conceptualisation common to European languages is that the future is a point in space that we are moving towards. The future is commonly constructed with 'I am going', or its equivalent. A feature of contemporary

French is that the grammatical future, 'je le ferrais' (I will do it) is becoming much less used than the going-to future, 'je vais le faire' (Fox, 1994). One cannot argue that this is happening because the going-to future involves less morphological complexity and less cognitive load. Language does not evolve according to a pattern of increasing grammatical simplification. A more consistent explanation can be found in the current strength of the schematisation of the future as a point we move towards and the prominent role that this is taking in the minds of contemporary French speakers. The reason why this should be so can only be a matter of speculation, but if we reflect on the extent to which contemporary Western civilisation has fostered the sense of an individual as able to control their own future, a plausible explanation presents itself.

More than at any time before, people in contemporary France are able to grow up with the belief that they can set their own life goals. They can visualise these, either from day to day or over a span of years. They can construct their lives as purposeful movement, not as the ploughing of a predestined furrow. The increasingly sophisticated concept of planning with such associated activities as organisational analysis and risk management posit an unparalleled extension of the horizons within which we can construct a life of goal-directed movement. Contemporary Western cultures are perhaps more than ever able to inculcate their members with the sense that they should plot their lives as goal directed movement, and so such a schematisation of time becomes more and more prominent. It would be surprising if this was not reflected in the construction of language.

Clearly, conceptual metaphor has a considerable role to play in the construction of language by culture and the transmission of culture as language. Furthermore, the effect of culture upon language is far from being trivial in the manner once assumed. This does not attest, however, to a straightforward and easily identifiable difference between the meanings located in one language and culture and another. Languages are built around conceptualisations that, even if they are not universal, are often shared among languages that derive from a common strand. In this way, lanaguages transmit the modes of thought that have evolved in ancient and lost cultures. Languages such as Latin, Spanish or English, by virtue of their association with expansionist colonial powers, may carry their inherited modes of thought across to colonised cultures while bending to new expressive needs, reworking the metaphors they inherit or extending them in new ways. If language cannot, therefore, offer a clear set of tribally demarcated meanings, the language teacher will wonder if a sense of conceptual metaphor will actually help them transmit the meanings of their students' target language. In order to answer this, I will recount a brief pedagogical episode, suggesting how a sense of conceptual metaphor could help a teacher to deal with the problem of meaning and the consequent error that arose.

A pedagogical example

The following episode shows how a failure to grasp meaning can arise from cultural preconceptions. It arose in a small class consisting of six adults with a wide variety of cultural backgrounds, embracing Europe, the Middle and Far East. To begin, I had asked the students to close their eyes and to find one of their earliest memories. I prompted them with questions about the sound the memory made and how the scene smelt. After a few minutes, I asked one student to describe the scene. Their description was quite bland:

> **Student:** 'I was walking with my mother. There was a path. The path was very long and I was tired. I wanted to go into my mother's back.'

I drew a box on the board with a figure going inside it, while putting another leaning against the outside. I wrote underneath the box: 'Into or onto?' and obtained the response, 'Onto my mother's back.' There was then an exchange about how in the student's country at that time a mother would carry a child 'in the back'. Therefore using 'go into' was not so much a misunderstanding of a preposition as a literal attempt to convey a cultural practice.

From the perspective just recounted, two explanations are possible. The first explanation focuses on the word 'in' and the second explanation focuses on the word 'back'. The use of 'in' generally contrasts with 'on'. 'In' suggests being enfolded by vertical space. 'On' suggests being surrounded by horizontal space. Yet the use of 'in' reflects how both these concepts are subject to extension. We talk about 'living in a country' without envisaging that nation as a kind of box that enfolds us. We say we are 'running in front of the race' without assuming that 'front' is a pit that we have fallen into before all our rivals. Further, through 'the time is space' metaphor, any spatial reference can have a temporal equivalent. Thus, 'I am there in June' treats the month as enclosing vertical space, whereas 'I am coming in a while', indicates an approximate point on a predefined, horizontal plane. In thus encapsulates a wide category of reference.

Prototypes

According to Rosch (1975, 1978), categories were not stable and consistent entities to which phenomena did or did not belong. Thus, we do not recognise robins, eagles and ostriches as birds because they share such features as beaks, wings and feathers. Further, we do not set up a bird category as meaning the sharing of the features, beaks, wings and feathers.

Rosch found categories to be anchored in cognition by a prototypical example. When studying how Americans formed the category of a bird, Rosch found that it was most often around the robin. The robin was central to their idea of what a bird was, with such species as the blue-jay, canary and blackbird, also being important. A species such as an ostrich was clearly peripheral, with the penguin and the bat ranked at the extreme edge of the class (Rosch, 1975). A category, then, is not a defining set of features that pre-selects which items belong to it and which do not. Lakoff (1987) develops this conception into a notion a radial category and extends the flexibility of the concept still further. Accordingly, the outlying members of a given category may not actually share any features with a central prototypical member. The nature of the prototype does not predict or predetermine the nature of all the other category members.

As is shown in Figure 1, the preposition 'in' sets up a spatial category. Prototypically, it instantiates the occupation of vertical space, the object in a box. As a teacher this was the meaning to which I made a reflexive reference when the word was misused. Yet as has been seen, the meaning extends to outlying instances that have less to do with this, situating us in respect of events whose spatial existence is in a permanent state of change. Figure 1 is very far from being an exhaustive account of 'in'. It makes the point about how an ostensibly straight-forward spatial category is extended in several complex ways. Another point that is remote from the prototypical concept would find that the word has been removed from the spatio/temporal domain altogether, perhaps via 'the state is location metaphor', to give us 'live in happiness'. My point is more to show how the construction of this category means that when a student wants to talk about carrying a baby in the back, they are being correctly motivated by their sense of the fluid construction of the category. They have supposed that the back of the mother could be a place in which the infant wants to find a protective niche. This extension could be the result of making the incorrect transfer of a schematisation that is allowable in their mother tongue because the equivalent preposition covers a different radial domain. It could also be the result of the student's own linguistic or metaphoric creativity making an incorrect extension of the domain of the English word 'in'.

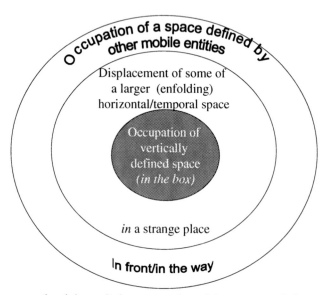

Figure 1 An example of the radial construction of the category 'in'

However, it might be that this error should not really focus on the over-extension of 'in' but of the noun that it precedes, 'back'. The student's insistence on there being a cultural justification for their misuse of the preposition suggests that the habit of carrying infants in a sling on the back has allowed the conceptual extension of back into the sling that rests upon it. We have either a conceptual metaphor 'a sling for carrying infants is the back it rests upon' or a metonymy where 'back' substitutes for 'sling'. The exact definition of metonymy is difficult but prototypically it may suppose one item, a sail, standing for another item with which it has a spatial or contiguous relationship, a ship, as in the sentence, 'I saw two sail'. Here the metonymy may arise from how the back is standing for the unmentioned sling and is contiguous to it.

In any linguistic realisation of metaphor or metonymy it is difficult to define where the figurative use of language ends and the literal begins. For example, in an idiomatic construction such as 'I was bowled over', the metaphor would appear to focus on the verb, 'bowled over'. However, in order for the referent of the first person pronoun to be subject to this emotional assault they must themselves be considered as a kind of skittle. The real location of the metaphor might be in the conceptualisation of the first person pronoun. This, in itself, makes an argument for metaphor being a conceptualisation which is reflected in language as opposed to a linguistic construction that can be identified through formal criteria. The exact location of the metaphor or metonymy may be an academic point, therefore. The interest of this type of construction lies in the underlying conceptualisation and in the cultural assumptions that may be motivating it.

Conclusions

In this article I have begun reviewing five of the ways that can justify the introduction of cultural content into the language curriculum. I have called these approaches the communicative view, the classical curriculum view, the deconstructionist view and the competence view. As my description implied, the first two approaches have serious flaws.

In its pure form, the communicative view makes unwarranted assumptions about the learner as a user of the target language. It asserts that the learner will use the TL in a set of situations that can be mapped out in advance. It makes little allowance for how the learner's own cultural background may determine the type of encounters that they are likely to have and the forms that these will take. It does not recognise that the meanings a learner may want to express are not an automated response to a given context but a product of the individual's cultural background and how that shapes their encounter with another culture. A given group of learners will not derive the meanings of the TL as a stable semantic system but according to the cultural preferences that every individual brings to bear and according to how these interact with the context in which the meanings are expressed.

The classical curriculum view does not require prolonged examination in an age of mass language learning. Students now learn languages for a host of reasons. The individual student must themselves decide whether or not their investment of time and intellect is given greater value by the interest of the culture to which the TL grants access. There is no deductible principle through which a given culture will confer more value on the language through which it is expressed. In an age of international languages and multi-cultures, culture itself can no longer be constructed as a monolithic entity able to add value to language.

The third, culture-free language view raises questions about the relationship of language to culture, which this paper partly tries to examine. It also raises the larger issue of whether science can be value-free, which is beyond the province of the paper, unless it is to observe that even if science is free of the values of a culture, scientific cultures will propagate the ethos of science, valuing observation and deduction. Further, the culture-free language view makes assumptions about an MT culture as being essentially fragile and at risk of contamination. The contamination issues from a TL culture which is assumed to be morally inferior although fashioned around superior technological and economic power. For many, language learning is partially about finding ways to counter such prejudices.

The deconstructionist and the competence view both give culture an important place in language teaching, because they see it as essential to the full grasp of meaning in the TL. Both positions assume a semantic relativism where meanings are not fully shared between languages and where this differentiation is a consequence of the effect of culture upon language. They therefore beg the question of whether, despite the universalist search for the common and significant primitives of meaning, culture does have such an effect. In order to answer this, I looked briefly at the discussion of this in the emerging discipline of cognitive linguistics. This inquiry did not support any overly straightforward picture of a coherent and indivisible culture infusing its language with its own eccentric areas of meaning. However, there is clearly room to show that language and culture influence each other within the formulation of conceptual metaphor and the construction of abstract thought that is its product. The picture is of a language as transmitting a collection of the schematisations of past users. Some of these will be universals, others will belong to the now remote cultures that contributed to the evolution of a contemporary culture. Language is thus a bearer of the past conceptualisations that may themselves have been culturally distinct. Yet language is also adaptable and constantly sensitive to the newer conceptual metaphors of the cultures to which it comes to give voice.

My final contention is that this relationship between culture and language is important to how teachers perceive language. In order to show how this was the case, I looked at the question of how English prepositions divide the category of direction. I then used the example of a student error with prepositions to show how this proceeded from a misunderstanding of how English schematised the area in question. This misunderstanding was culturally motivated in that it arose from a way of carrying children. My conclusion is that such insights do not simply enhance the teacher's awareness of the origins of student errors. They also furnish strategies with which the teacher can expose to the student how their target language divides up the territory of meaning. One can first help students to understand 'in' or 'back' as representing a category of meanings. One can next give students an insight into the principles that lie behind the extension of the prototype, thus inviting them into the conceptual core of a language and perhaps leading them towards the more successful manipulation of its semantic system.

Correspondence

Any correspondence should be directed to Dr Randal Holme, Department of Linguistics, University of Durham, Durham, DH1 1TA, UK (h.r.holme@durham.ac.uk).

References

Byram, M. (1989) *Cultural Studies in Foreign Language Education*. Clevedon: Multilingual Matters.
Byram, M., Esartes-Sarries, V. and Taylor, S. (1991) *Cultural Studies and Language Learning: A Research Report*. Clevedon: Multilingual Matters.
Byram, M. and Fleming, M. (eds) (1998) *Language Learning in an Intercultural Perspective: Approaches Through Drama and Ethnography*. Cambridge: Cambridge University Press.
Byram, M. and Risager, K. (1999) *Language Teachers, Politics and Cultures*. Clevedon: Multilingual Matters.

Chomsky, N. (1965) *Aspects of the Theory of Syntax.* Cambridge, MA and London: M.I.T. Press.

Dudley-Evans, T. and St John, M.J. (1998) *Developments in ESP: A Multi-disciplinary Approach.* Cambridge: Cambridge University Press.

Fairclough, N. (1989) *Language and Power.* London: Longman.

Fox, A. (1994) *Linguistic Reconstruction: An Introduction to Theory and Method.* Oxford and New York: Oxford University Press.

Gibbs, R. (1992) Why idioms are not dead metaphors. In C. Cacciari and P. Tabossi (eds) *Idioms: Processing Structure and Interpretation* (pp. 57–78). Hillsdale, NJ: Erlbaum.

Gibbs, R. (1994) *The Poetics of Mind.* Cambridge: Cambridge University Press.

Goatly, A. (1997) *The Language of Metaphors.* London: Routledge.

Grady, J. (1997) Foundations of meaning: Primary metaphors and primary scenes. PhD Thesis, University of California, Berkeley.

Halliday, M.A.K. (1985) *An Introduction to Functional Grammar.* London: Edward Arnold.

Halliday, M.A.K (1993) Some grammatical problems in scientific English. In M. Halliday and J. Martin (eds) *Writing Science* (pp. 69–85). Pittsburg: University of Pittsburg Press.

Heine, B. (1997) *Cognitive Foundations of Grammar.* Oxford: Oxford University Press.

Hodge, R. and Kress, G. (1993) *Language and Ideology.* London: Routledge.

Johnson, K. (1982) *Communicative Syllabus Design and Methodology.* Oxford: Pergamon.

Johnson, M. (1987) *The Body in the Mind: The Bodily Basis of Meaning, Imagination and Reason.* Chicago: University of Chicago Press.

Kress, G. (1989) *Linguistic Processes in Socio-Cultural Practice.* Oxford: Oxford University Press.

Lakoff, G. (1987) *Women, Fire and Dangerous Things: What Categories Reveal about the Mind.* Chicago: University of Chicago Press.

Lakoff, G. and Johnson, M. (1999) *Philosophy in the Flesh.* New York: Basic Books.

Lakoff, G. and Johnson, M. (1980) *Metaphors We Live By.* London and Chicago: University of Chicago Press.

Maybin J. (ed.) (1994) *Language, Literacy and Social Practice: A Reader.* Clevedon and Philadelphia: Multingual Matters in association with the Open University.

Núñez, R., Neumann, V. and Mamani, M. (1997) Los mapeos conceptuales de la concepción del tiempo en la lengua Aymara del norte de Chile (Conceptual mappings in the understanding of time in Aymaran language of Northern Chile). *Boletin de Educación de la Universidad Católica del Norte* 28: 47–55.

Phillipson, R. (1992) *Linguistic Imperialism.* Oxford: Oxford University Press.

Roberts, C., Byram, M., Barro, A., Jordan, S. and Street, B. (2001) *Language Learners as Ethnographers: Introducing Cultural Processes into Advanced Language Learning.* Clevedon: Multilingual Matters.

Rosch, E. (1975) Cognitive representations of semantic categories. *Journal of Experimental Psychology (General)* 104, 192–233.

Rosch, E. (1978) Principles of categorisation. In E. Rosch and B. Lloyd (eds) *Cognition and Categorisation* (pp. 27–48.) Hillsdale: NJ: Lawrence Erlbaum.

Street, B. (1996) *Literacy, Culture and Development.* Cambridge: Cambridge University Press.

Thompson, G. (1996) *Introducing Functional Grammar.* London, New York, Sydney and Auckland: Arnold.

Whorf, B.L. (1956) *Language, Thought and Culture: Selected Writings of Benjamin Lee Whorf.* New York: Wiley.

Wierzbicka, A. (1980) *Lingua Mentalis.* New York: Academic Press.

Wierzbicka, A. (1986) Does language reflect culture? *Language in Society* 15 (3), 349–373.

Wierzbicka, A. (1997) *Understanding Cultures through their Key Words: English, Russian, Polish, German and Japanese.* New York and Oxford: Oxford University Press.

Autobiographical Contexts of Mono-Cultural and Bi-Cultural Students and their Significance in Foreign Language Literature Courses

Christiane Fäcke
Universität Bremen, Fachbereich 10, Postfach 330440, 28334 Bremen, Germany

In this paper I discuss the latest development of an empirical project about the mental processes of students with both mono-cultural and bi-cultural socialisation in foreign language literature courses. Introspective methods help to analyse how students tackle Antonio Skármeta's *No Pasó Nada* (1980), in which he describes the way of life of a young Chilean refugee living in Berlin. Which mental processes happen while reading this text? What significance do autobiographical factors have? Which contexts do the students evoke? Starting with a description of the project itself and the empirical methods applied to the study of students following a Spanish course, I will concentrate on the mental processes and autobiographical contexts of two students. Then, I will discuss the importance of autobiographical contexts by analysing two utterances that show how perturbation can take place. The research methods are influenced by ethnography of speaking, conversation analysis and discourse analysis.

Intercultural Understanding and Foreign Language Literature

Discussions with students about literary texts often show that they react quite differently. Once, after having read a novel, a student told me in an interview that she was quite interested in the main character's relationships with some of his friends at school while another student did not even remember these characters. The other student was interested in the romantic element, while the first student could not even remember the names of the lovers. Why is the same text received so differently?

This observation was the starting point of this empirical study which deals with forms of intercultural understanding by foreign language literature students. It focuses on the mental processes of single students with a mono-cultural or bi-cultural socialisation. The central question concerns the influences of mono- and bi-cultural socialisation on the attitudes and mental processes of students in foreign language literature courses in an intercultural context. How do these students discuss literary texts and their contents? In which ways are they interested in and open-minded to intercultural understanding?

The context of this study is different texts of foreign language literature in which certain subjects such as foreignness, culture, identity and migration are discussed (cf. Wendt, 1996b). These literary texts are regarded as the context of the learning situation. In a first study, I analyse the mental processes of pupils in a Spanish course and their reading of Antonio Skármeta's *No Pasó Nada* (1980). Which mental processes happen while working on this text, while reading it? What significance do autobiographical factors such as country of origin, life experience and resulting attitudes have in that context?

Skármeta tells the story of the 15-year-old Lucho who fled with his parents and his younger brother from Pinochet's dictatorship in Chile. Since then, they have been living in exile in Berlin. There is no difference between Lucho and other young people in as far as he goes to school, plays soccer, falls in love and fights with other young boys. At the same time, there are cultural borders because repeatedly Lucho talks about differences between Berlin and Santiago de Chile. He also has intensive contacts with members of other minorities. His best friend is a young Greek boy whose family have also left their home country for political reasons. Lucho also joins other Chileans on occasions of political opposition in exile.

The centre of the story is a conflict between Lucho and Michael, a young German. Although Lucho is much afraid, the two finally meet to fight against each other on an isolated yard of a factory. There they fight till they drop. The distance between the German and the Chilean gets smaller with each blow to the head they exchange. At the end of this unusual intercultural learning process, there is a friendship full of solidarity, and Michael goes to a meeting of the Chile Comité.

In order to investigate the intercultural understanding of foreign language literature students when confronted with this text, and in particular the relation between socialisation and mental processes (Nold, 1996; Ofteringer, 1995; Steinke, 1999), introspective methods (Faerch & Kasper, 1987) were selected. We planned to validate these introspective methods by triangulation (Flick, 1992; Henrici, 2001). Think-aloud-protocols (Mißler, 1993; Nunan, 1992), diary studies (Bailey & Ochsner, 1983) and interviews (Bock, 1992; Kruse & Schmidt, 1998; Küppers, 1999) were selected to offer both an introspective and a retrospective view. As members of a group reading the novel in class, the students were asked to read part of the text individually and think aloud about it. After the class teaching, they were asked to discuss several questions focusing on their retrospective reflections on the text. And throughout the reading process, they were asked to keep a personal diary.

In the following section I describe the findings of the first study carried out in what will eventually be a large project involving several courses of foreign language literature in a Gymnasium in the Rhein-Main-Area (Frankfurt). So far, the first study involving four students on a Spanish course has been completed.

The following description focuses on two of these students, who participated voluntarily in the study. First, they needed to get used to the think-aloud situation and the interview format. This familiarisation was easily accomplished. More problematic were the diaries: some students maintained their personal diaries consistently as they were reading, others were less consistent. The following extracts and summaries of the introspective data were selected by the analyst. They concentrate on utterances in which the students refer to certain autobiographical contexts.

Introspection and Retrospection

Isabel

The student presents herself as follows. Isabel, 20 years old, lives in a small town near Frankfurt, migrated from Spain to Germany at the age of 7. Her nationality is Spanish, her L1 is Spanish, she prefers to speak Spanish but thinks she speaks German better (higher linguistic competence and more possibilities to express herself). Her parents are both Spanish, speak Spanish at home and hardly speak German. They migrated to Germany as immigrant workers. Her father is a factory worker, her mother a housewife. Isabel wants to study psychology but fears that she will fail the university entry exam.

Isabel says that she is interested in personal and social aspects of the text. She doesn't have any problems with understanding it. First of all, the text seems to be funny, amusing and entertaining. She notes that it's written in an ironical and thought-provoking way.

> Also es wird alles so ein bisschen ins Lustige gezogen und auch wenn man manchmal grad so eher nachdenklich ist, kommt dann irgendwas und es bringt einen wieder zum Lachen. Also man lacht da eher drüber, es ist irgendwie witzig geschrieben, wenn's irgendwie krass klingt, aber das… die ganze Situation, also das mit dem Telefonat, als er mit dem Michael da redet, das klingt alles irgendwie so… das ist einfach, als würden die die ganze Zeit nur so rumshaken, also Spaß machen, obwohl es ja eher schon ernst ist. Also ich find das Buch sehr gut, ich find's sehr gut. [I'm amused by reading it, it's funny in a way… but the whole situation, when they talk on the phone… they seem to make fun even when it's serious. I think the book is very good. Note: The English glosses are not literal translations, but rather a summary of what is said.]

She sees Lucho as a nice young boy, and she interprets Michael's behaviour in terms of racism. She talks about this in a very emotional and empathic way. She says that racism is an important subject to her, that it can't be verified directly in the text but that there are many allusions to it. But when Michael is talking to Lucho by phone and when he says 'escucha chileno', this is hard. In other words, Lucho does not like the fact that his nationality is mentioned, and he is hurt.

> … es wird schon zum Teil auch Rassismus angesprochen, weil dieses *escucha chileno*, dieses hör mal, das ist so irgendwie… das drückt irgendwie Rassismus aus… weiß ich nicht, das kommt mir jetzt grad so vor, da war vorher im Text schon mal so'ne Stelle gewesen. Und diese Nationalität, die angesprochen wird, dass er aus Chile ist, … ich glaub das ist auch das, was ihm sehr weh tut, also da hat er… gefällt ihm überhaupt nicht. [It also deals with racism, because *escucha chileno* expresses racism. Thus his nationality becomes a source of pain.]

Isabel notices especially Lucho's father because of the discrepancy between his deep interest in Chile and his lack of interest in his family. She bases her assumptions about the father's attitudes on her observations of his emotional character, his national pride and his machismo. She notes that his family is less important to him, but is also surprised by the father's pride in his son during the demonstration for Chile.

Isabel talks about differences between Germans and Chileans and characterises the Germans as being reserved and the Chileans as being open. She also talks about the Chilean vocabulary which is difficult to understand because some of the Chilean words are unknown in her native country, Spain.

Ich denk, viele Wörter sind drin, die... die man jetzt auch aus dem Spanischkurs oder als Spanier gar nicht kennen kann. Die sind irgendwie so aus Chile so ein bisschen halb Chile, ein bisschen halb Spanisch, also versteht man nicht so ganz, kennt man vielleicht auch in Spanien gar nicht so, aber es ist gut zu verstehen, es ist witzig und unterhaltsam. [There are many words that we can't know from our Spanish. They come from Chilean Spanish, but it's entertaining and easy to understand.]

Asked about the main theme of the text, Isabel names several themes – Chile, the generation gap, exclusion from society. When I ask Isabel if she would recommend the text for other courses she says she found the text very good because it familiarises people with the background of Chilean history. Isabel notes that the text sets you thinking, it is interesting to read, it includes much Chilean vocabulary, it makes you wish to continue reading. She says that the text invites reflections about how foreigners feel in Germany. Most of the time, someone looks from his own perspective, not noticing the difficulties of the parents, for example, in finding a new job and getting used to living in another society. Isabel is aware that Lucho's parents have more problems than Lucho himself because it is easier for younger people to fit into a new situation than for older people.

Ich find, der Text bringt einen zum Nachdenken wie sich... wie sich Ausländer hier fühlen in Deutschland, wie man sich, wenn man selbst hier Ausländer ist, fühlt, äh... wie sich dann auch die Eltern fühlen. Weil meistens geht man von seiner eigenen Situation aus, wie fühle ich mich in 'nem anderen Land, aber man geht gar nicht davon aus, wie schwer es die Eltern haben in 'nem anderen Land, 'nen anderen Job zu kriegen und äh einem selber dann auch äh... essen geben zu können, Kleidung, alles was man braucht. Man geht immer von sich selber aus, wie komm ich in 'ne neue Schule, was mach ich da und ... da merkt man halt in dem Text, dass es auch den Eltern halt nicht so gut geht und in dem Beispiel da sogar den Eltern viel schlechter geht als Lucho, weil als junge Person kommt man ja eher mit 'ner fremden Umgebung klar als ältere Leute. [I think the text sets you thinking how strangers feel in Germany, how you yourself think when you're a foreigner... and how parents feel. Usually you think about your own situation, clothes, school, etc. You learn from the text that parents have even more problems than Lucho, because as a young person you fit more easily into a new situation than older people.]

So Isabel mentions her bi-cultural background several times when she talks about the text and her ways of interpreting it. She says that she is very interested in the text, its content and subject matter, that it is about many important subjects of everyday life and that everybody can put themselves in the position of a Chilean in Berlin, no matter what their national affiliation.

Also ich find den Text, wie soll ich sagen... ich find er ist irgendwie... ich glaub er behandelt halt viele wichtige Themen, auch Alltagsthemen, in die sich jeder hineinversetzen kann, also jetzt nicht nur Leute, die aus Chile kommen, sondern egal aus welchem Land, auch Deutsche können sich hineinversetzen, jeder. Das ist irgendwie... die Nation ist egal, aber es ist irgendwie... er behandelt halt wirklich ziemlich viele Themen, aber irgendwie auf ironische Weise. [The text deals with many important subjects that everybody can understand, not only Chileans but also Germans. Nationality doesn't matter.]

Thomas

The student presents himself as follows: Thomas, 18 years old, with two sisters at home, his father working in a bank, his mother working as a nurse twice a week. They live in the same town near Frankfurt as Isabel. His hobbies are gliding, life-saving in swimming pools, the cinema, music, meeting friends, working in the school library. He wants to be a pilot or maybe to study physics.

Thomas has been learning Spanish for three-and-a-half years and in the beginning was very interested in it. Then he lost his motivation for a while. Now, however, he is interested in it again because of his new Spanish teacher's style and because Spanish seems to him more relevant than Latin and French.

First of all, Thomas reflects about methods of understanding a text, not about the text's topic. His interest in the Spanish course is concentrated first of all on foreign language acquisition, on understanding an unknown text with little guidance and on learning vocabulary. He explains his difficulties with the different style of teaching for beginners and for advanced learners and with the unknown vocabulary. He has learned how to handle these situations by changing his method of reading the text. He has stopped searching for every unknown word in the dictionary and now looks up every second word he cannot guess. He has not achieved global understanding of the text so he tries to discuss the content with other students in order to avoid misunderstanding. Only passages of direct speech, however, are easy for him to understand.

Thomas talks negatively about the text. He justifies this attitude by saying that the content is uninteresting and that there are too many words whose meanings he does not know. The text contains too many abstract and philosophical elements. He identifies two topics, integration and conflict resolution between young people.

In general, he found the text boring and, apart from a few aspects, did not like it very much. He thinks he did not learn anything new while reading it. Maybe the story itself was an enrichment, but he did not see its relation to current affairs. Thomas noted that other stories with immigrants were more up-to-date than this text.

> ...'ne Bereicherung war's schon ja,... aber dass ich jetzt viel daraus jetzt so neu gelernt hab, eigentlich weniger. Es war eigentlich mehr so 'ne story, also 'ne Geschichte, die ich so für sich betrachtet hab, und die jetzt nicht so irgendwie aktuell... äh... beziehen konnte, ja... Ich denke mal, da gibt's vielleicht andere Geschichten auch mit Immigranten, die da vielleicht bisschen aktueller sind oder... aktuelle Themen damit zeigen. So als Geschichte kann man es lesen, klar... wenn man sich bisschen dafür interessiert, aber es ist halt nicht mehr das Aktuellste... [Well, it was an enrichment... but I did not really learn anything new. It was just a story, but there could be other stories with immigrants that are more up-to-date.]

Thomas mentions his surprise and his disappointment about the end. The fight seems to be strange to him and he had expected a diplomatic solution. He puts himself in the position of the main characters and compares their behaviour with his own. Thomas is surprised that Lucho behaves so kindly to Michael after the fight. Lucho waits until Michael wakes up and then helps him. Thomas said that if he had been in Lucho's situation, he would not have helped him.

> Ich hab mich gewundert... oder nee gewundert hat's mich eigentlich nicht, dass er dann... dass dieser Lucho dann auf den Michael, dass er darauf gewartet hat, dass er wieder wach geworden ist... ja kann man das so sagen?... Ich hätt's wahrscheinlich anders gemacht. Ich hätt ihn dann wahrscheinlich liegen gelassen, weil wenn mich jemand angreift, ja, okay, es ist natürlich idiotisch erstmal in diese Situation zu kommen, aber angenommen ich wär in dieser Situation ja, ich würd mich von jemandem aufm Motorrad mitnehmen lassen, um irgendwo hinzufahren ja, es ist nicht meine Art ähm... dann würde ich demjenigen, wenn er am Boden liegt, würd ich sagen: okay, hast halt gelitten, ja das war's denn halt... [I would not have done the same as Lucho. Perhaps I would have cleared off. It's idiotic to be in this situation, this is the way things are.]

The story, therefore, has a happy ending, in that the two characters try to understand each other. Thomas expected another ending, understanding by communication and not by fighting. Maybe Michael understood that it is senseless to solve a conflict that way.

> ... dass er [Lucho] versucht, mit ihm zu kommunizieren. Deswegen hatte ich mir auch gedacht, die werden sich anderweitig einigen ja. Ich hab da, also hätte ich 'ne Wette abschließen können, dass die sich nicht kloppen ja, wo ich den Autor jetzt gar nicht kenne, hätt mir das Ende anders gedacht. Gut: happy end kann man eigentlich schon sagen, mehr oder weniger, dass... da die sich ja im Nachhinein dann ähm... verstehen wollen. Aber ich sag mal, der Michael hat auch keine andere Wahl gehabt... [I thought they would react in another way. I would have bet that they wouldn't have fought. Well it's a happy ending, they want to understand each other. Michael did not have a choice.]

He believes that there must be a didactic interest or purpose of teaching in the text. One could learn that conflicts can't be solved by fighting. Then, he questions his own reflections.

> Vielleicht hat er auch eingesehen, dass es alles sinnlos ist, dass man Konflikte halt nicht so auf die Art lösen kann, dass sie nicht dadurch veschwinden, sondern dass die halt nur durch andere Wege verschwinden. Ich mein, dass könnte ein Grund sein, warum dieser Text grad für'n Unterricht genommen wird (lacht), da stecken ja immer so'n paar Absichten dahinter, ja... aber ob das jetzt nun Einfluss auf nen Schüler hat, der jetzt in Spanisch, das Fach das er freiwillig gewählt hat, ob das jetzt nen pädagogischen Wert hat, weiß ich nicht. [Maybe he accepts that conflicts cannot be solved that way. I mean, there could be a reason to use this text for teaching, there are always aims. But I don't think that this can influence students.]

Thomas compares linguistic aspects of the story. He talks about his four-week stay in foreign countries on holidays and compares his experiences to Lucho's situation in Berlin. He says that it is always difficult to be in another country, for the Chileans in Germany as well as for himself in other countries in Europe. Thomas notes that it is more difficult to speak a foreign language in the foreign country itself than in a foreign language course.

> … ja mit der Sprache vielleicht noch was, ähm… es ist halt immer schwer, wenn man in ein anderes Land reinkommt und man kann die Sprache nicht so gut. In dem Fall konnte er… konnten die Chilenen das überhaupt nicht, ja, die konnten keine deutsche Sprache, doch der Junge – falsch – der Junge hat das ja in der Schule gelernt, fällt mir grad wieder ein. Ich war auch schon ein paar Mal im Ausland, jetzt so europamäßig, und es ist schon schwierig, 'ne Sprache halt im Ausland zu sprechen. Das ist was anderes, als wenn man das im Unterricht so macht, wobei das jetzt nicht so in dem Buch behandelt wurde. Ist mir jetzt nur so eingefallen… [It's always difficult in a foreign country with the language. The Chileans did not speak German, but the boy had learned it in school. I was in foreign countries in Europe, too, the real thing is always different.]

Autobiographical Contexts Mentioned by the Students

After this description, I will analyse the ways in which Isabel and Thomas discussed their experiences while reading this text in their Spanish course. Which autobiographical contexts did they mention and in what way did they relate this story to their own lives?

Isabel refers indirectly and directly to her country of origin, Spain, for example, by mentioning linguistic differences between the Spanish spoken in Spain and in Chile. She compares her experiences in Spain and in Germany. She talks about cordiality, intensive social contacts and vivacity in Spain, and about the Mediterranean temperament that knows little distance. She refers to her own experiences with cultural standards. At the same time, she mentions Germany, and the aloofness and coolness of the German people. She says that she can sympathise very well with the Chileans because of her experiences in Spain. She mentions racism several times but discusses it only vaguely. She talks about feeling foreign in Germany and about the tasks and problems of parents and of children. She classifies these subjects as very important and supposes them to be important for everyone, regardless of national affiliations.

Thomas refers to other personal points. He compares Lucho's life and his own and mentions his holidays, which were overshadowed by his own problems with foreign languages in foreign countries. He talks about his difficulties learning a foreign language and compares his situation as a tourist in a foreign country with Lucho's life in Berlin. He puts himself in Lucho's place and underlines the differences in behaviour between Lucho and himself. He opts for diplomatic solutions and for communication instead of fighting. To sum up, Thomas looks at Lucho and his family from a certain distance. He has an outsider's approach to Lucho and he pities him when he is left by his girlfriend.

Isabel and Thomas both refer to autobiographical contexts. Isabel evokes the context of being a member of an ethnic minority, the context of her country of origin, the context of living as an immigrant in Germany. She often alludes to these categories even though she voices universalist interpretations about the text ('everybody can understand the topic').

Thomas also refers to autobiographical contexts, of being a young boy who can identify with Lucho through the fight, the context of being a member of the majority in Germany with an outward approach to the topics of immigration and integration and the context of being a young boy who has experience of sometimes violent rivalries with other young boys.

Isabel and Thomas choose as starting points certain autobiographical aspects of their identities as male and female and as members of an ethnic majority or minority. They both talk about their own experiences, both individual events and repeated experiences. While Isabel tends to evoke less gender-oriented perspectives and more culture-oriented ones, Thomas tends more towards gender-oriented ones.

Mental processes and autobiographical contexts

What about the significance, the importance and the meaning of those autobiographical contexts? What about their influence on the mental processes of the students? I would like to answer these questions by analysing the ways in which Isabel and Thomas discuss autobiographical contexts in two exemplar utterances in their interviews.

Thomas mentions what he expects from Lucho whom he expects to have difficulties with several aspects of the host culture, including the climate and the expectation of punctuality in Germany. He notices that Lucho doesn't correspond to that in the text, but this discrepancy does not lead Thomas to question his expectations.

Ich hab mir schon gedacht, dass er jetzt, wenn er nach Deutschland reinkommt, o je, was wird er denn jetzt... wie wird er sich da jetzt verhalten... die leben ganz anders, die leben alle nach der Uhr, exakt nach der Uhr. Pünktlichkeit ist angesagt in Deutschland... das kann ich mir gut vorstellen, dass da halt... nicht einfach ist. Hm... das ist in dem Buch, hm, ich überlege, ist das in dem Buch gut genug behandelt? Er hat ja jetzt kein einziges Mal geschrieben, dass er jetzt zum Beispiel zum Unterricht zu spät gekommen ist, ja, das hätte vielleicht dann in dieses Bild, das ich mir so vorstelle, noch reingepasst, dass er vielleicht mal Ärger mit 'nem Lehrer bekommen hat hier. [I was wondering about the way how Lucho would behave in Germany. The punctuality in Germany must be difficult for him. I don't know if this is mentioned well enough in the book. He never wrote that, for example, he was late for school. Well this would have been consistent with what I think about it.]

Isabel is different from Thomas. She also shows some degree of cultural bias. She focuses in particular on a conversation between Lucho, his German girlfriend, Edith, and her father. This father appears to be very kind and open-minded and he welcomes Lucho like a Chilean. After having noticed this, Isabel is quite irritated because of her experiences in Spain, where cheerful welcomes are usual. For this reason, Isabel believed, when the conversation had ended it was also Edith's father (a German), who said goodbye to Lucho. In fact, it was Edith who kissed Lucho goodbye.

> Er [Lucho] wird dann auch gleich eingeladen zum Essen, ich glaub da ist er auch ganz stolz drauf und… jetzt hab ich nun nicht mitbekommen, von wem er jetzt geküsst wird, ich… ich glaub vom Vater… (zögert, liest lang) ich zweifel jetzt… (liest) nee (flüsternd) … (lacht), nee, ich glaub das ist doch die Edith, die das macht, und da ist er jetzt auch ganz schüchtern und wird ganz rot, ja… stimmt… hätt ja auch nicht sein Vater sein können. [Lucho gets an invitation for dinner. But now I did not get who kisses him, I… I believe it was the father (hesitates)… I doubt it… no… no… it's Edith and he is quite timid and he blushes.]

While Thomas doesn't revise his constructions in reaction to the text, the irritation Isabel experiences seems to be too important for her to ignore. For example, she modifies her construction about the identity of the German father who behaves like a Chilean and about the person who is kissing Lucho.

The autobiographical context, therefore, seems to be a very important factor for Isabel and Thomas in the reading of this text. They both start with personal experiences that are quite dominant. Their autobiographical contexts lead to a certain selective perception. Their existing stereotypes are not easily revised. Challenges to the reader's sense of order or identity are not evident while reading the text.

We may therefore conclude that the reader's autobiographical background seems to facilitate a personal approach to the text and influences the interpretation of it. Apparently, it gives occasion to make hypotheses for one's own constructions of how to come to an understanding of the text. The students appear both implicitly and explicitly to reflect their identities in their personal statements. This confirmation of their personal values far outweighs the appearance of new constructions that are consolidated through the text. In appearance, new constructions are a sign of a modified understanding and of an awakening mental process through challenge. Depending on the nature of their autobiographical starting points, the students appear to choose different contexts for their interpretation of the text, the subject or the content. The identification with single starting points seems to aid understanding or to facilitate an empathetic approach. The students can also demonstrate indifference or the wish to keep a distance.

Conclusion

The constructivist theory of learning (von Glasersfeld, 1995) helps to explain the results. According to this theory, students initially recognise in a text aspects of their own experiences. They make viable their constructions of reality and revise them if necessary (cf. Wendt, 1996a: 66). Learning is seen as the development of cognitive systems by trial and error whose purpose is individualisation and socialisation.

The examples of the mental processes of Isabel and Thomas show how single students open themselves to new constructions or not and how individualisation and socialisation are constructed. In this process, the *individuum* and his/her biography seem to be very important. Thomas and Isabel initially recognise aspects in the text that correspond with their own constructions. The bases of their understanding are the relationships they construct between their own existing constructions and constructions that correspond to them in the text. This demonstrates that new information can lead under certain circumstances to self-doubt and to new constructions (cf. Wendt, 1996a).

This initial approach to the mental processes of students has shown the importance and the significance of autobiographical contexts and their influence on the reading and understanding of text.

Correspondence

Any correspondence should be directed to Dr Christiane Fäcke, Universität Bremen, Fachbereich 10, Postfach 330440, 28334 Bremen, Germany (faecke@firemail.de).

References

Bailey, K.M. and Ochsner, R. (1983) A methodological review of the diary studies: Windmill tilting or social science? In K.M. Bailey, M.H. Long and S. Peck (eds) *Second Language Acquisition Studies*. Rowley, MA: Newbury House.

Bock, M. (1992) Das halbstrukturierte-leitfadenorientierte Tiefeninterview. Theorie und Praxis der Methode am Beispiel von Paarinterviews. In J. Hoffmeyer-Zlotnik (ed.) *Analyse Verbaler Daten. Über den Umgang mit Qualitativen Daten*. Opladen: Westdeutscher Verlag.

Faerch, C. and Kasper, G. (eds) (1987) *Introspection in Second Language Research*. Clevedon: Multilingual Matters.

Flick, U. (1992) Entzauberung der Intuition. Systematische Perspektiven-Triangulation als Strategie der Geltungsbegründung qualitativer Daten und Interpretationen. In J. Hoffmeyer-Zlotnik (ed.) *Analyse Verbaler Daten. Über den Umgang mit Qualitativen Daten*. Opladen: Westdeutscher Verlag.

Von Glasersfeld, E. (1995) *Radical Constructivism: A Way of Knowing and Learning*. London: Falmer Press. (Studies in Mathematics Education Series, 6).

Henrici, G. (2001) Zur Forschungsmethodologie. In H. Vollmer, G. Henrici, C. Finkbeiner, R. Grotjahn, G. Schmid-Schönbein and W. Zydatiß *Lernen und Lehren von Fremdsprachen: Kognition, Affektion, Interaktion. Ein Forschungsüberblick. Zeitschrift für Fremdsprachenforschung* 12 (pp. 1–145).

Kruse, A. and Schmidt, E. (1998) Halbstrukturierte Interviews. In G. Jüttemann and H. Thomae (eds) *Biographische Methoden in den Humanwissenschaften*. Weinheim: Psychologie Verlags Union.

Küppers, A. (1999) *Schulische Lesesozialisation im Fremdsprachenunterricht. Eine explorative Studie zum Lesen im Englischunterricht der Oberstufe*. Tübingen: Narr. (Giessener Beiträge zur Fremdsprachendidaktik).

Mißler, B. (1993) *Datenerhebung und Datenanalyse in der Psycholinguistik*. Bochum: AKS.

Nold, G. (1996) Die Analyse kognitiver Verstehensstrukturen in verschiedenen Tätigkeitsbereichen des Fremdsprachenunterrichts. In G.W. Schnaitmann (ed.) *Theorie und Praxis der Unterrichtsforschung. Methodologische und Praktische Ansätze*. Donauwörth: Auer.

Nunan, D. (1992) *Research Methods in Language Learning*. Cambridge: Cambridge University Press.

Ofteringer, I. (1995) Wie begegnen Schülerinnen und Schüler einem fremden Text? In L. Bredella and H. Christ (eds) *Didaktik des Fremdverstehens*. Tübingen: Narr.

Skármeta, A. (1980) *No Pasó Nada*. Barcelona: Pomaire.

Steinke, I. (1999) *Kriterien Qualitativer Forschung. Ansätze zur Bewertung Qualitativ-empirischer Sozialforschung*. Weinheim, München: Juventa.

Wendt, M. (1996a) *Konstruktivistische Fremdsprachendidaktik. Lerner- und*

Handlungsorientierter Fremdsprachenunterricht aus Neuer Sicht. Tübingen: Narr. (Giessener Beiträge zur Fremdsprachendidaktik.)

Wendt, M. (1996b) Zum Thema 'Fremdheit' in Texten für den spätbeginnenden Spanischunterricht. In: H. Christ and M.K. Legutke (eds) *Fremde Texte Verstehen. Festschrift für Lothar Bredella zum 60. Geburtstag.* Tübingen: Narr.

Learning Culture by Communicating: Native–Non-Native Speaker Telephone Interactions

Gisèle Holtzer
Université de Franche-Comté, Faculté des Lettres et Sciences Humaines, 30 rue Megevand, 25030 Besançon CEDEX, France

This paper reports on a research programme (the SCOTLANG program) set up to study the development of L2 interactive skills and sociocultural competence among English and French native speaker university students as evidenced in a communicative context. The preliminary findings reported here concern the acquisition of informal register by L2 speakers and the handling of topic development in native–non-native speaker telephone conversations. In addition, the exolinguistic nature of the bilingual interactions leads to L1–L2 code-switching as native speakers assist non-native speaker comprehension. Other L1–L2 code-switching phenomena are described but not yet accounted for at the present early stage of the project.

The SCOTLANG research program is based on the study of interactions between Scottish students from the University of Stirling learning French and French students from the University of Franche-Comté Besançon learning English. The basic hypotheses were that the interactions between a language learner and a native speaker could have three positive effects: communicative, cultural and affective. When using the foreign language in the natural contact situations of telephone and e-mail interaction (although in this paper only telephone communication is reported on), the learner has the status of an active player responsible for carrying out a range of communication tasks: managing the transmission of appropriate meaning, contributing to the exchange, and ensuring, with the other participant, the construction of coherent discourse. It was anticipated that the contact situation would put the learners in the position of 'cultural speakers' by requiring them to adjust their beliefs and values and to understand those of the other (Byram & Zarate, 1997). With this aim, a set of conversation topics was prescribed (immigration, stereotypes, student life in France and Scotland, etc.) so as to encourage exchanges of opinions and stimulate 'the cognitive processes of comparison and discussion' (Neuner, 1997: 73). It was also anticipated that inter-action with a native speaker would have a positive influence on the learners' perception of their own ability to use the foreign language to communicate and their motivation to continue learning it. As will be clear, these hypotheses are based on the objectives identified by the Council of Europe and investigated by the SCOTLANG program as a European project.

The experiment was conducted within an institutional framework. Specifically, the student informants were paired by the teaching staff of the two institutions who also prescribed a (non-exhaustive) list of conversation topics before the exchange began. The frequency and the duration of the conversations (one weekly contact lasting 20 minutes) were also prescribed, as were the procedures to be followed (a recording of each conversation was to be made and a learning diary was to be kept). Thus, the interactions were programmed and guided as part of an institutional teaching project in which the students were committed to the weekly interactions as a component of their language learning programme. They were informed that the purpose of this contact with native speakers was to help improve their oral skills and cultural competence.

Conversation and Topic Control

As the exchanges were both controlled by the institution (external determination) and linked to the subjective behaviour of the participants (internal determination), they could be considered 'semi-natural'. They were therefore expected to manifest some of the characteristics of natural conversation, defined by Kerbrat-Orecchioni (1990) as having the following characteristics:

- non-formal in character (familiar, spontaneous, improvised) and without obvious external compulsion. Conversations are casual talk in everyday settings in which nothing is established beforehand, be it topic, duration or other components;
- having as its main objective the pleasure of chatting for chatting's sake;
- being egalitarian in nature: conversation functions on the basis of equality between participants who behave as if they were on an equal footing: 'A conversation is marked by the relative equality of its participants – or more correctly, by the participants behaving as if they were equals' (Donaldson, 1979: 279). In this experiment, equality was founded on the identity factors of similarity – age, status, sex (almost all the participants being female).
- conversation is focused on contact and the affirmation of interpersonal relations.

In the interactions, the informal aspect is shown in the use by the French students of a colloquial register or style (for example, *ouais* instead of *oui*, *c'est pas évident* (dropping the double negative marker, *ne*). Improvisation is marked by hesitations, repetitions and incomplete sentences typical of discourse that is being constructed in real time. Thus, the Scottish students when learning French are in contact with the authentic target language as used in social interaction. This places them in the position of having to react to language used for communication. However, improvisation is not applied to the content of the exchange since the topics were established beforehand, and thus topic development is in the realm of the foreseeable. Contrary to what takes place in natural exchanges, the introduction of a topic in these exchanges is usually explicit. Stating the topic (a reminder of the common task) is typically followed by its confirmation by the other participant, a confirmation which may or may not be accompanied by a comment:

Example 1

French speaker **(FS):**   Donc aujourd'hui on doit parler des stéréotypes

                            (So today we've got to talk about stereotypes)

Scottish speaker**(SS):**   Oui, c'est un topic très difficile

                            (Yes, it's a difficult topic)

Example 2

SS: Euh le sujet aujourd'hui est le logement

   (The subject today is housing)

FS: Le logement oui

   (Yes housing)

In a natural conversation, topic management occurs as the conversation progresses, with changes of topic, breaks, redirections and digressions typically manifested. However, the flow of the conversation is underscored by a coherence principle that authors writing on the 'art' of conversation as long ago as the 18th century considered to be an essential quality of all conversation. Abbey Morellet (1812), taking his inspiration from Swift's *Hints Towards an Essay on Conversation*(1710), maintained: 'Conversation must be neither rigorously methodical nor completely disconnected' (Fumaroli, 1997: 434). Thus, natural interactions are flexible and characterised by the presence of discourse and other markers (*à propos, tiens, alors, what about, I say, well*) which direct the listener in the interpretation of the topic as it develops in the conversation; according to Goffman (1981), these forms are makeshift links or bridges which are applied as needed. They show compliance on the part of the speaker with the need for coherence when the connection with what went before is less obvious.

A change of topic initiated by the native speaker can pose a risk for the non-native speaker. The use of discourse markers, which are often not perceived by the listener, is not really of much help to the non-native speaker. Thus, when a new topic is introduced by the native speaker, it can lead to lack of comprehension. In the following example, the topic under discussion is the town of Toulouse with its university and Mediterranean climate. Without warning, the FS introduces a new topic. The coherence is not made clearly apparent by the discourse markers *sinon* (if not) and *à part* (besides) which a native speaker would have been expected to recognise as indicating an explicit change of topic.

Example 3

FS: Sinon qu'est-ce que tu aimes faire à part tes études?

   (If not what do you like to do besides studying?)

SS: Je n'ai pas compris

   (I didn't understand)

FS: Tes... ce que tu aimes?

   (What do you like?)

SS : J'aime beaucoup aller au cinéma

   (I like going to the cinema)

And in the following example, the subject of the exchange was historic events in Scotland and France (William Wallace, the Dreyfus affair) when the FS started on a new topic introduced by *mais* (but)

Example 4

FS: Mais tu apprends le français depuis combien d'années?

(But how many years have you been learning French?)

SS: Pardon?

(Sorry?)

FS: Tu tu apprends le français depuis combien de temps?

(How long have you been learning French?)

SS: A douze ans

(Since I was 12)

Acquiring Sociocultural Competence

Examples (3) and (4) show that although the broad topic had been established beforehand, the management of the content of the conversation left considerable room for improvisation by the participants. To the extent that it is predictable, communicative activity gives the non-native speaker the possibility of planning contributions and preparing the specific vocabulary and structures that are to be used. However, the possibility of improvisation brings about unpredictable aspects; the learner is obliged to mobilise communication resources and use a range of communication strategies to maintain the exchange.

One of the aims of the SCOTLANG project is to develop the students' ability to react spontaneously in real time to the unforeseeable nature of interactions. Thus, the communicative autonomy of both participants in the interaction needs to be assessed.

Communicative competence includes the linguistic manifestation of sociocultural competence as evidenced by appropriate interaction rituals (excusing, thanking, etc.), use of adjacency pairs (such as greetings), politeness phenomena, formulaic expressions and other idiomatic or 'set' phrases such as *t'attends le train?* (what are you waiting for), *y a pas de sot métier* (one job is as good as another), *à chacun son métier et les vaches seront bien gardées* (each to his trade and the work will be well done), etc. Such expressions are cross-culturally variable even between apparently similar cultures. As Kerbrat-Orecchioni states, 'Variations are to be found everywhere' and affect, in particular, spontaneous conversation whose meaning is often thought obvious by the speaker but appears opaque to the non-native addressee: variations 'can intervene and affect all aspects and be found at all levels of interaction' (1994: 15).

Our initial analysis indicates that the Scottish learners of French are progressively acquiring certain rituals, such as those that govern the opening of telephone conversations. This opening gambit takes place according to a well-established routine: summons–identification–salutation/greeting (Schegloff, 1972, 1986). Example 5 illustrates this routine.

Example 5

FS: Allo

(Hello)

SS: C'est Stéphanie?

(Is that Stéphanie)

FS: Oui bonjour James how are you?

(Yes, hello James, how are you)

SS: Très bien très bien et toi ça va?

(Fine, just fine, and how are you)

FS: Oui très bien merci merci

(Yes just fine thanks)

To be integrated into a foreign language speech community is also to understand what are, in a given culture, the appropriate techniques to carry out certain communicative tasks such as, for example, how to bring up a topic in a natural way. Our study of informal conversations in French has shown that topics are introduced by a great variety of short phrases at the beginning of the conversation. Some are metalinguistic (*alors, à propos*; well, what about) and others phatic (*dis donc, tu sais, écoute*; hey, do you know, listen). Sometimes both types are combined in the same utterance (*oh dis, à propos, tu vas à la réunion demain?*; Oh I say, what about the meeting tomorrow, are you going?). Formal teaching usually pays very little attention to this category of expression and its pragmatic function. Direct contact with the foreign language in informal situations appears to familiarise students with these culturally specific expressions.

Code-Switching in Exolingual-Bilingual Interaction

The communication situation in which the student pairs find themselves is an exolingual-bilingual one. An 'exolingual' interaction is 'any verbal interaction that is characterised by significant differences between the respective linguistic repertoires' of the participants (Alber & Py, 1985: 35). The typical context is where a non-native speaker communicates in the language of a native speaker partner.

Exolingual communication is usually asymmetric or unequal in both linguistic and cultural respects with the native speaker occupying the position of the expert in the interaction. The exolingual parameter introduces an inequality factor into an interaction that is by definition egalitarian (see above). The extent of this inequality varies according to the level of competence of the non-native speaker. It is still too early to assess with any accuracy the importance of this parameter in the Besançon-Stirling interactions, but we are already able to show that it has an effect on communication strategies and encourages a more cooperative behaviour, with native speakers overlooking the linguistic or cultural mistakes of non-native speakers and assisting their less competent partners (see Example 6 below).

The contact situation is also bilingual. Every language learner is a bilingual who progressively builds up a bilingual repertoire. The French and Scottish students share knowledge of two languages, one of which is both a mother tongue and a foreign language for the other. However, because the institutional framework prescribes a structure (the exchange must be in French for the first 10 minutes and in English for the following 10 minutes), the conversation is not expected to exhibit code-switching of the kind usual in bilingual interaction. Rather, what is anticipated is two monolingual conversations, one conducted in French and one conducted in English. However, our data show that this prescription is rarely scrupulously adhered to so that the 'monolingual' interactions frequently show the (limited) bilingual ability of the participants, with code-switching used as a communication strategy.

Tarone (1980: 419) defined communication strategies from the interactive point of view and focused on the cooperative criterion: 'The term relates to a mutual attempt of two interlocutors to agree on a meaning in situations where requisite meaning structures do not seem to be shared.' This approach seems to direct attention to communication troubles or problems of comprehension which force the participants to try to agree on the meaning of the problematic contributions to their exchange. Hence, in a blocked situation, it would seem natural to resolve communication problems by means of another shared language. Thus, in the following example, switching to English is part of a cooperative strategy in response to a silence which appears to the native speaker to signal the non-native speaker's lack of comprehension.

Example 6

FS: J'ai un petit frère de 24 ans. Tu comprends?

(I've a younger brother who is 24. Do you understand?)

SS: Oui

(Yes)

FS: Qui vit à Singapour

(Who lives in Singapore)

<silence>

FS: Singapour Singapore

SS: Oh oui

(Oh yes)

Here the native speaker used code-switching as a strategy to assist the non-native speaker to recognise a lexical item (the French word is replaced by its English equivalent). Such examples of code-switching as a communication strategy are relatively common in exolingual-bilingual interactions. We suspect that they are much less frequent in the language classroom where such strategies are rarely accepted.

Not all instances of code-switching can be explained so easily, however. Consider the following example:

Example 7

FS: Je vais aller à Edinbourgh au mois de juillet

(I'm going to Edinburgh in July)

SS: Combien de temps?

(For how long?)

FS: Deux semaines two weeks je suis leader assistant tu comprends? Je dois I must be in contact with the cooperation and supervise the students

SS: Tu vas visiter Glasgow?

(Are you going to visit Glasgow?)

FS: Non je dois rester I must stay in Edinburgh for two weeks et j'espère I hope to visit Glasgow for two days I hope

SS: Glasgow est une belle ville

(Glasgow is a beautiful city)

In this sequence, where French is the designated language of communication, the intervention of the native speaker is in the form of long fragments in English in a discourse where French is reduced to a couple of utterances. There are translations or alternating repetitions which are apparently not motivated (*deux semaines two weeks, je dois rester I must stay*). The non-native speaker is either respecting the contract or wants to speak the target language as much as possible and does not change languages or code-switch. How, then, can the mixing of languages by the native speaker be explained? Is it a preventive strategy? Does he believe that the transmission of his message in French would make it less comprehensible for his partner? Is this a conscious or unconscious way of placing himself at the same linguistic level as his partner to reduce the differences between them? The researcher remains uncertain.

Conclusion

The SCOTLANG program is based on an active and interactive perspective: the user-learner of a foreign language is a social player who uses her receptive and productive L2 communication skills in interactive situations with another social player who is a native speaker of the target language. In this exercise, using real language in real time, an interaction is built up by both players. One consequence is that the development of the linguistic competence of the user-learner depends to some degree on the contribution of the native speaker participant. This leads to a problem that can only be mentioned in passing, that of how to assess the learner-user's linguistic gain, available for observation as it is in a natural interaction. The preparation of appropriate descriptors for measuring this gain is one important feature of the project which is still to be undertaken.

Correspondence

Any correspondence should be directed to Dr Gisèle Holtzer, Université de Franche-Comté, Faculté des Lettres et Sciences Humaines, 30 rue Mégevand, 25030 Besançon CEDEX, France (gisele.holtzer@univ-fcomte.fr).

References

Alber, J-L. and Py, B. (1985) Interlangue et conversation exolingue. *Cahiers du Département des Langues et des Sciences du Langage de l'Université de Lausanne* 1, 30–48.

Byram, M. and Zarate, G. (1997) Définitions, objectifs et évaluation de la compétence socioculturelle. In *La Compétence Socioculturelle dans l'Apprentissage et l'Enseignement des Langues* (pp. 7–42). Strasbourg: Conseil de l'Europe.

Donaldson, S.K. (1979) One kind of speech act: How do you know we're conversing? *Semiotica* 28 (3&4), 259–99.

Kerbrat-Orecchioni, C. (1990) *Les interactions verbales* (tome 1). Paris: A. Colin.

Kerbrat-Orecchioni, C. (1994) *Les interactions verbales* (tome 2). Paris: A. Colin.

Fumaroli, M. (1997) *L'Art de la Conversation.* Paris: Dunod.

Goffman, E. (1981) *Forms of Talk.* Philadelphia: University of Pennsylvania Press.

Neuner, G. (1997) Le rôle de la compétence socioculturelle dans l'enseignement et l'apprentissage des langues vivantes. In *La Compétence Socioculturelle dans* l'Apprentissage et l'Enseignement des Langues (pp. 43–124). Strasbourg: Conseil de l'Europe.

Schegloff E. (1972) Sequencing in conversational openings. In J.J. Gumperz and D. Hymes (eds) Directions in Sociolinguistics. New York: Holt, Rinehart and Winston.

Schegloff, E. (1986) The routine as achievement. Human Studies 9, 111–51.

Tarone, E. (1980) Communication strategies, foreigner talk and repair in interlanguage. Language Learning 30, 417–31.

Exporting Methodologies: The Reflective Approach in Teacher Training

Ana Halbach
Universidad de Alcalá, Colegio San José de Caracciolos, C/Trinidad 3, 28801 Alcala de Henares, Spain

In the field of English language teaching there seems to be a generalised tendency to accept and use teaching methodologies and textbooks in certain contexts that have been developed in and for a different context. Recently, this rather unquestioning use of methodologies has been challenged (see, for example, Holliday, 1994), with authors pointing out that what might be suitable for one situation might not be equally so for a different one. Thus, it would seem to be more fruitful to try to establish the appropriateness of what has been imported and, if necessary, make the suitable changes and adaptations, so as to make most of the methodology. This is precisely the aim of the present paper, which explores the extent to which a reflective approach to teacher training is suitable for teaching undergraduate students a course in methodology at the University of Alcalá in Spain, and, if not, what kind of changes will make it more fruitful in this specific context.

Although in teacher training courses several methodologies can be followed, in the past few years, with an increasing awareness of the fact that teaching is a highly complex, context-dependent skill, a reflective approach to teacher training (see Wallace, 1991) has been given preference (see, among others, Richards, 1990; Ur, 1997). This approach, which originated mainly in the English-speaking countries, has been adopted in countries all over the world, including Spain. At our university, we follow this approach with the aim of, among others, giving trainees tools for reflection on classroom practice, a critical understanding of what is at stake in teaching English as a foreign language, and an awareness of the underlying theoretical principles for the methodological options, rather than providing them with specific techniques and skills. In principle, this would allow our students to become reflective and critical about issues related to methodology, while at the same time enriching their own previous 'personal theory' of teaching.

However, the idea of 'exporting' methodologies from one country (and culture) to another has recently been challenged, since the idea that if one methodology is effective in one context it will also be so in another ignores the importance of personal and cultural factors in learning. Thus, it has been pointed out several times that autonomous learning, for example, may be suitable for Western societies, but will face many problems in Eastern cultures (see, for example, Benson, 1997; Pennycook, 1997; Sinclair, 1997). Following these ideas, it also becomes necessary to look at whether the reflective approach in teacher training is really suited to other cultures and contexts.

In this paper I am going to analyse whether or not our students in Spain become more critical and more reflective through the way in which they are taught, or whether this methodology does not really have an effect on the way they think about teaching. To do so I will draw on different sources of information, such as the work students produce during the course, students' answers to an attitude scale dealing with basic issues in the teaching / learning process at the beginning and at the end of the course, and their comments in the student diaries they keep for the course. The data I will analyse were gathered from students from various courses.

The Study

The course under study is the subject of methodology as taught to undergraduate students of English at the Universidad de Alcalá (Spain). Methodology is an optional subject whose aim is on the one hand to familiarise students with the main issues in the methodology of foreign language teaching, and at the same time to help them reflect critically on the contents they are exposed to so as to be able to enrich their own personal theory of language learning. Students are assessed by means of a combination of a diary and an end-of-term paper (see Halbach, 1999a,b for further information about this).

The data about the extent to which students are able, at the end of the course, to reflect critically and whether or not they have gained and internalised the knowledge about methodological options presented in the course comes from different sources. The first of these sources is the diary students have to keep for their course. In it, students are asked to reflect along very general guidelines about the issues dealt with in the course, ask questions about them, relate these issues to their own experience as language learners, discuss the pedagogical implications of the ideas presented, and generally, enrich the contents of the course through their own critical thinking (see Porter *et al.*, 1990: 228–229 for a similar list of guidelines). Two aspects of students' work are important for the information they yield about the effect of the course on their ability to think critically: the type of reflection they are able to produce, and whether or not they comment on the methodology followed in the course.

As far as the type of reflection is concerned, following Jarvis's (1992) model, three degrees of reflection are distinguished:

(1) *Summarising*: Students summarise the ideas talked about in class, give a rather general evaluation of these ideas, reach conclusions that are not backed up by anything in the text, and generally don't show a significant degree of introspection or reflection.

> Today, we had to explain, by groups, things that can influence the learning. My group had to explain how personality affects the way of learning. (Student 11, 20.2.)

(2) *Exemplifying*: Students relate the contents of the course to their own experience, providing examples and anecdotes, and show a certain degree of introspection in relation to their own language learning experience.

> Now I know the importance of the pre-reading activities; I never did this kind of activity, but activating background knowledge is very important and helps the student to understand better. (Student 2, day 9)

(3) *Commenting*: Students pose questions which are more or less closely related to the contents of the course, they reflect about various issues related to language learning and teaching, and in general their comments show a

change in awareness and in their understanding of the process of language teaching/learning.

> This seems a complaint diary more than a reflection one. The thing is that now I've got the elements to criticise the methods I've never liked. (Student 4)

The type of reflection that appears most frequently, especially in the later parts of the diary, is thought to give an indication of how successful students have become at thinking about issues related to methodology.

This ability to reflect critically should be complemented by a raised awareness of issues related to methodological choices in general. Thus, if students comment on the methodology they are experimenting with in both their course in Methodology and in the other subjects they are taking, they are not only showing that their awareness is raised, but also that they understand and are able to reflect on the way courses are set up. This last aspect, the reflection, is especially important given the great influence the methodology followed in teacher-training courses seems to have on students' own beliefs. However, the fact that issues related to the methodology followed in the course are mentioned is not by itself a guarantee for good reflection to be taking place, as can be seen in the following comment, which doesn't really move beyond a general evaluation that doesn't seem to be based on analysis or reflection:

> I have felt that it was interesting the technique of snowball groups. I think it is a way of sharing information, but in a 'participatory' way. (Student 5, 27.2.)

The second set of data is related to the change in students' general perception and valuation of the issues related to language teaching and learning during the course and consists of students' answers to an attitude scale questionnaire based on the one designed by Karavas-Doukas (1996), which was administered at the beginning and end of the course (see Appendix for the questionnaire). The idea behind using this tool is that students who have entered a cycle of reflection during the methodology course are likely to have enriched their own personal theory of teaching. This personal theory of teaching would then reflect some kind of bias towards a more communicative language teaching, since this is the approach favoured in the course in Methodology. Reflection is necessary for this, since:

> reflection may be a precondition for intake to enter the teacher change cycle, through which it will be processed at an increasingly deep and personal level to become part of the teacher's system of values and classroom behaviours. In this way, the intake to the teacher change cycle becomes uptake which is eventually represented in teaching outcomes (Pennington, 1996: 343).

This change of attitude towards teaching, for which reflection can be taken to be a necessary precondition, is also reflected in the end-of-term paper students have to produce, especially in those which centre around the design of an activity to develop one of the four communicative skills. If this activity is in line with the principles underlying communicative language teaching, the author will probably have gone through a process of meaningful reflection on the issues presented to him/her in the course, so that they have indeed become uptake.

Results

Judging from the type of reflection students are able to carry out at the end of the course, out of the 23 students who kept a diary during the academic year 00/01, only nine produced entries which reflect their own critical thinking. The rest of the students stayed at the level of exemplifying, with only two of them having summarising as the predominant mode in the entries. Generally speaking, this reflects a low level of critical thinking among the students.

In relation to the methodology used in the course or in other subjects students were taking at the same time, only a few students consistently comment on this aspect with more than just a sweeping evaluation. Not commenting on this aspect means, on the one hand, that they are missing out on an important source of information and/or reflection, and on the other that somehow their awareness towards methodological questions has not been raised sufficiently, thereby not allowing them to think about and analyse what they see.

It also became apparent that, generally speaking, there was quite a high proportion of students whose attitudes to language teaching/learning showed little change as a result of the work done in the course. Thus, in a study carried out with the same type of group during the academic year 98/99 (see Halbach, 2000), it was seen that the rate of change was quite low. Additionally, if we look at the lesson plans some of the students produced at the end of the course as their term-paper, we also find that about half of them did not reflect the premises of communicative language teaching the methodology the teacher training course clearly is oriented towards. Thus we find that students, for example, still include a lot of grammar work when trying to set up reading and/or listening activities and are not clear about the function of pre-reading and/or pre-listening activities.

Discussion

All in all, judging from the evidence summarised in the previous section, it seems that somehow most students are not prepared to enter into a cycle of reflection. This cycle would, on the one hand, allow them to analyse and reflect critically both on what they experience and on the topics discussed in class, and on the other, produce work that integrates some of the basic premises of language teaching presented throughout the course. Two possible reasons for this spring to mind. On the one hand, in this last academic year it became clear that those students who arrive at a good reflection are also those who have a better level of English, so that it might be the case that the fact that the whole teaching (including the work produced for the course) is carried out through the medium of English somehow constitutes a handicap for some of the students. This would be similar to the 'threshold level' Cummins (1979) postulated for the use of learning skills by bilingual students. The low level of proficiency in the foreign language is, however, also a problem in itself, since the students we are talking about are future teachers of English. This question thus leads us into a field which has implications for the whole system of university entrance requirements and of the level of degree courses generally, and which therefore far exceeds the scope of the present paper.

The other possible reason for the difficulties with reflection lies in the Spanish educational system which follows a rather transmission based mode of teaching, where little space is left for critical thinking. This impression is confirmed by a small survey into students' educational background, which showed that most of the successful students (8 out of 9) had a different educational background which, as they say, has had some influence on the way they study and probably let them experience a learning mode based more on critical thinking than on transmission. It seems that most of the students tend to feel very insecure when asked to analyse something and come up with their own ideas about it. One of their main worries is to give the 'right' answers, as can be seen in the following comment one of the students made in her diary:

> The last time you told me that my entries were very short (and I know that they were very boring too). The reason is not a low or nil interest on the subject, it is not that I feel annoying when I write; no, the truth is that I am afraid to be wrong. (Student 11, 6.3.)

Thus it seems that, owing to the students' educational background, the reflective approach may not be suited to a Spanish learning environment. However, this conclusion would imply abandoning this approach and thereby losing all the benefits it has in terms of empowering teachers by establishing the foundation for their own continuing development and helping them to adapt to new teaching contexts, among others. This would mean paying quite a high price, and would imply missing an opportunity to broaden students' learning experience, and therefore, rather than changing the whole methodology, I'd like to propose an 'acculturated' mode of reflective teacher training.

What students with this kind of background seem to need is greater scaffolding that will, first of all, start them off on their reflection and secondly, by giving them positive experiences of reflection, make them more self-confident when it comes to expressing their own ideas. What follows then, are a few measures that might contribute to making reflection more accessible for students.

First of all, although students are given some general guidance as to what should go into their diaries, it might be a good idea to make this guidance more specific, at least at the beginning of the course. This could be done by singling out a few points in each of the sessions and asking students to focus on them in their diary entries for that day, or by posing even more direct questions about some of the more controversial points. This would prevent students feeling lost when they first start keeping their diaries, and don't really know what they are expected to do.

Another thing that might prove useful is raising students' awareness of the new ideas they have been confronted with in a session by asking them to write down two or three things they have learned in that session. It often seems that students don't integrate new ideas into their previous understanding because they are not even aware of the differences between what they held true at the beginning of the session and the ideas that have been presented during the session.

Because of this difficulty of becoming aware of the differences between their previous thoughts and the new ideas introduced in the course, it might also be helpful to have students plan a lesson, activity or the like based on their implicit beliefs before being confronted with the new ideas and then let them revise it at the end of the unit. Initially this revision should lead to changes if students have become aware of the implications of what has been discussed for actual class-room practice. If these changes fail to appear it would be the teacher's task to draw the students' attention to it.

Generally speaking, since students are not used to thinking for themselves and to analysing the practical implications and the underlying assumptions of the issues dealt with, it may be necessary to monitor their performance more closely than would otherwise be done. It is not a question of correcting the exercises they carry out in class, but rather of making students think about the things they are producing, thus guiding their thoughts and, hopefully, enabling them to become more critical.

Finally, since the methodology employed in the course itself seems to exert an important influence on students' attitudes, and the reflection on it is likely to establish the necessary link between theory and practice, it might be worth drawing students' attention to this factor. This can be done either through direct questioning about their feelings and/or reactions towards the methodology used or, more generally, by drawing their attention to how classes have been set up.

All of these techniques are in principle opposed to the idea of allowing students to develop their own personal theories of teaching and/or enrich the existing ones, since all of them include a certain degree of guidance and prescription, and thus an underlying message of there being right and wrong answers. For this reason, these measures should be seen as something temporary to help students overcome a difficulty and, like all good scaffolding, should be removed little by little so that students can become more independent.

Conclusion

Like others before it, this short study points out some of the problems that can appear when a given methodology that has been developed in a certain context is transplanted from this context into another, without adapting it to the peculiarities of this new context. Attention has to be paid to cultural and personal factors, but also to students' educational background and factors that in principle are not directly related to the methodology such as the students' level of proficiency in the language which serves as a medium for instruction. This does not, however, mean that methodologies must not be exported or that they only have a local value, but rather that they have to be adapted so as to suit local characteristics.

Correspondence

Any correspondence should be directed to Dr Ana Halbach, Universidad de Alcalá, Colegio San José de Caracciolos, C/Trinidad 3, 28801 Alcalá de Henares, Spain (ana.halbach@uah.es).

References

Benson, P. (1997) The philosophy and politics of autonomy. In P. Benson and P. Voller (eds) *Autonomy and Independence in Language Learning* (pp. 18–34). Harlow: Addison Wesley Longman.

Cummins, J. (1979) Linguistic interdependence and the educational development of bilingual children. *Review of Educational Research* 49, 222–51.

Halbach, A. (1999a) Using trainee diaries for assessment: Type of entry and technical terminology. *The Teacher Trainer* 13 (2), 3–7.

Halbach, A. (1999b) Using trainee diaries to evaluate a teacher-training course. *ELT Journal* 53 (3), 183–90.

Halbach, A. (2000) Trainee change through teacher training: A case study in training English language teachers in Spain. *Journal of Education for Teaching* 26 (2), 139–46.

Holliday, A. (1994) *Appropriate Methodology and Social Context*. Cambridge: Cambridge University Press.

Jarvis, J. (1992) Using diaries for teacher reflection on in-service courses. *ELT Journal* 46 (2), 133–43.

Karavas-Doukas, E. (1996) Using attitude scales to investigate teachers' attitudes to the communicative approach. *ELT Journal* 50 (3), 187–98.

Pennington, M.C. (1996) When input becomes intake: Tracing the sources of teachers' attitude change. In D. Freeman and J.C. Richards (eds) *Teacher Learning in Language Teaching* (pp. 320–48). Cambridge: Cambridge University Press.

Pennycook, A. (1997) Cultural alternatives and autonomy. In P. Benson and P. Voller (eds) *Autonomy and Independence in Language Learning* (pp. 35–53). Harlow: Addison Wesley Longman.

Porter, P. *et al.* (1990) An ongoing dialogue: Learning logs for teacher preparation. In J. C. Richards and D. Nunan (eds) *Second Language Teacher Education* (pp. 227–40). Cambridge: Cambridge University Press.

Richards, J. C. (1990) Preface. In J. C. Richards and D. Nunan (eds) *Second Language Teacher Education* (pp. ix–xii). Cambridge: Cambridge University Press.

Sinclair, B. (1997) Learner Autonomy: The cross-cultural question. *IATEFL Newsletter*, October-November, 12–3.

Ur, P. (1997) The English teacher as a professional. *The English Teaching Professional* 2, 3–5.

Wallace, M. J. (1991) *Training Foreign Language Teachers: A Reflective Approach*. Cambridge: Cambridge University Press.

Appendix: Questionnaire

Read the following statements and rate them from 1 to 5, 1 standing for 'I strongly disagree' and 5 standing for 'I strongly agree' with 3 being the neutral rating.

(1) Grammatical correctness is the most important criterion by which language performance should be judged.

(2) Group work activities are essential in promoting genuine interaction among students.

(3) Grammar should be taught as a means to an end and not as an end in itself.

(4) Since the learner comes to the language classroom with little or no knowledge of the language, he/she is in no position to suggest what the content of the lesson should be or what activities are useful for him/her.

(5) Training learners to take responsibility for their own learning is useless since learners are not used to such an approach.

(6) For students to become effective communicators in the foreign language, the teachers' feedback must be focused on the appropriateness and not the linguistic form of the students' responses.

(7) The teacher as 'authority' and 'instructor' is no longer adequate to describe the teacher's role in the language classroom.

(8) Group work allows students to explore problems for themselves and thus have some measure of control over their own learning.

(9)   The teacher should correct all the grammatical errors students make. If errors are ignored, this will result in imperfect learning.

(10) It is impossible in a class of 30 students to organise your teaching so as to suit everybody's needs.

(11) Knowledge of the rules of a language does not guarantee the ability to use the language.

(12) Group work activities take too long and waste a lot of valuable teaching time.

(13) Since errors are a normal part of learning, much correction is a waste of time.

(14) The teacher as a transmitter of knowledge is only one of the many different roles he/she must perform in the course of a lesson.

(15) By mastering the rules of grammar students become fully capable of communicating with a native speaker.

(16) For most students language is acquired most effectively when it is used as a vehicle for doing something else and not when it is studied in a direct or explicit way.

(17) Tasks and activities should be negotiated and adapted to suit students' needs rather than imposed on them.

(18) Students do best when taught as a whole class by the teacher. Small group work may occasionally be useful to vary the routine, but it can never replace sound formal instruction by a competent teacher.

(19) Group work has little use since it is very difficult for the teacher to monitor the students' performance and prevent them from using their mother tongue.

(20) Direct instruction in the rules and terminology of grammar is essential if students are to learn to communicate effectively.

(21) A textbook alone is not able to cater for all the needs and interests of the students. The teacher must supplement the textbook with other materials and tasks so as to satisfy the widely differing needs of the students.

Think about your answers for a moment. Who or what has influenced your ideas about teaching? (Adapted from Karavas-Doukas, 1996).

'We Would Have to Invent the Language we are Supposed to Teach': The Issue of English as Lingua Franca in Language Education in Germany

Helene Decke-Cornill
Universität Hamburg, Fachbereich Erziehungswissenschaft, Von-Melle-Park 8
20146 Hamburg, Germany

The focus of English language teaching is changing from a concern with English-speaking countries, especially Britain and the United States, to the role of English as a lingua franca. The impact of this change on understanding of teachers of English concerning the nature and aims of their subject in the school curriculum was explored through interviews with teachers in German schools. Teachers with strong academic qualifications teaching in a selective school (*Gymnasium*) rely more heavily on a focus on specific countries and cultures than those in a non-selective school (*Gesamtschule*), who often have no specific academic qualifications in English. The latter are more at ease for themselves and their learners with the concept of English as a lingua franca than the former, although they share some of the doubts about standards and models of language competence to guide their teaching. If English is indeed to be taught as an international language, however, there are implications for teacher education and the need to re-consider the traditional Humboldtian view of the relationship between language and culture.

The Role of English in German Schools

In the course of the last 15 years or so, English, already firmly established before as the most prominent foreign language in education by far, has gained additional ground in curricula in Germany. English is now taught in most primary schools, has become compulsory in vocational training, has taken the place of most Russian classes in former East Germany, and has become the most important language in the increasing field of teaching other subjects through the medium of a foreign language, a field that used to be dominated by French until the late 1980s. Although English is broadly accepted and its increase usually welcomed with enthusiasm, there are some reservations with regard to its increasing dominance. Sceptics fear its effect as 'killer language' on other established school languages such as French and Latin as well as on languages of migrant communities such as Turkish, Italian, Polish and Russian whose delicate hold in primary education is endangered while English flourishes. According to them, early English and English as a first foreign language threaten multilingualism, and they suggest that English should be left until a later stage, well after another foreign or second language is introduced.

Whereas the spread of English in education during the 1960s was motivated by the Cold War and the economy of the Western Alliance, its recent further rise must be seen in the context of globalisation in general and European Unification in particular.[1] As far as the latter is concerned, its official policy favours linguistic diversity, but its inner logic and economy counteract the official programme. The balance between a common language and multilingualism has become a matter of rising concern which I have discussed elsewhere (cf. Decke-Cornill 1999, 2001; see also Breidbach, this issue). The 'European Year of Languages' in 2001 indicated an awareness of that tension: it supported initiatives against an impending reduction of national, local and migrant languages to home languages without, however, questioning the need of a lingua franca.

Because of its history, English has had a headstart on other European language to serve as that lingua, and today – despite many critics, including native speakers of English – its function as a link medium between speakers of different languages seems established. It is this potential that has fostered English since the mid-1980s and given it its prominence in German language policy. Chancellor Gerhard Schröder voiced a widely shared view in education policy when he asked for English to become a compulsory second language from the first years of primary school (see 'Stellungnahmen: Englisch ab der 1. Klasse', *Die Woche* 17, 21 April 2000).

Thus, the shift towards English as lingua franca (ELF) has affected the spread of English in education. But has it also affected the substance and the objectives of English language teaching? The post-war focus of the English classroom in Germany was Britain, whose language, culture, life and institutions were at the centre of teaching and learning. From the 1960s onwards, the USA was added – albeit reluctantly by those who considered the New World unworthy of educational attention. Later on, one or two units on Australia were also included into the textbooks. With the present move towards internationalisation, however, this national perspective needs to be reconsidered. 'Eine *lingua franca* muß als *lingua franca* gelehrt werden' ['A *lingua franca* must be taught as *lingua franca*'], Werner Hüllen pointed out 15 years ago (1987: 58).

Two or three years ago, I started asking newcomers to my seminars about their experience with ELF. As far as their English lessons at school were concerned, none of them remembered the lingua franca function playing any significant part. The same applied to their university studies as future English teachers. English teacher education in Germany continues very much in a national tradition. Its core subjects are English or American studies, sprinkled with the occasional post-colonial and immigrant writing.[2] The language is British or – to a lesser extent – American English, with a glimpse at other Englishes here and there. Near-nativeness remains the aim, and nativeness in that context relies heavily on the idea of a standard, the overall implication being that English teaching ought to prepare for communication with native speakers of standard English.

Thus, it appears that at this point in time, the case of English both as a school subject and as a subject of teacher education is rather contradictory. Its expansion is officially justified because of its international scope while its teaching remains locked into a nationalist, culture-specific tradition. English in German education is torn between the local and the global, the territorial and the non-territorial.

Teachers' Perspectives on ELF: Findings from Two Staff Interviews

In the spring of 2001, I investigated this issue with the English staff of two schools in Germany to find out what teachers think about it. I decided to have problem-centred, semi-structured group interviews (Flick, 1995: 94–114) with the staff as a group, and not with the individual staff members, for two reasons. First, it is the group of teachers as a whole that gives a subject its profile in a school. Second, I had discovered previously that group interviews can be much more productive than individual ones because of the mutual inspiration between the participants.

The two schools where the interviews took place were rather dissimilar. One is a *Gesamtschule* (Comprehensive School) in Hamburg with multicultural and multilingual classes – a dozen or more different linguistic and cultural backgrounds in one class is no exception. The pupils enter at the age of 10, after primary school, and leave at the age of 16, at the end of compulsory schooling. The English staff consists of 10 teachers. Half of them do not hold a university degree in English. This is not unusual. When required, quite a few teachers in *Gesamtschulen* or *Hauptschulen* in Germany teach subjects they did not study at university. The other school is a *Gymnasium* (Grammar School) in Potsdam, formerly East Germany, with pupils aged between 11 and 19. These pupils take the *Abitur*, the examination for university entry, at the end of upper secondary schooling. Only a tiny minority come from immigrant families. The English staff I interviewed comprised six teachers, all with a university degree in English.

Gesamtschulen and *Gymnasien* have a very different history. The latter has a long tradition which goes far back into the 19th century, when Greek and Latin were its core languages. It was only at the end of the 19th century that modern languages were reluctantly integrated into this type of élite school for the upper classes, on condition that they were taught in the manner of the classical languages, with a strong focus on grammar and translation. *Gesamtschulen*, on the other hand, are non-selective. They originate from the educational reform of the 1960s which aimed at a more democratic school system that offered all children the opportunity of higher education, no matter what their social background.

Both interviews lasted about an hour and a half. The participants each filled in a short questionnaire about their university background and their subjects. After a brief introduction to the topic, I conducted the interviews on the basis of the following questions:

- What do you think about the impending shift from a culture-specific to a global focus of English language teaching?
- In what manner does/would this shift affect the language classroom?
- Do you feel you already include lingua-franca-specific elements in your teaching?
- Does/would an ELF focus influence your identity and motivation as English teachers?
- With a view to ELF, in what way should English teacher education change?

Views expressed by both the Gesamtschule and the Gymnasium staff

All the teachers, without exception, emphasised their wish to open up the minds of their students for the diversity of people and cultures and expressed their hope to instil interest in different ways of living and thinking. Respect for heterogeneity featured prominently in their professional self-concept.

> For me, the value of language teaching is to make the children aware that people do not only speak differently, they also think differently. And that one ought to respect people who think differently and speak differently. And that one can gain something on the way. (*Gymnasium* teacher)

> What is important is that there is some development, that one becomes more open and aware of risks. That communication means taking risks: Watch out, misunderstanding ahead! (*Gesamtschule* teacher)

Considering the significance of ELF in curricula and public statements, it was surprising to learn that none of the teachers in either groups had ever explicitly reflected on this issue.

> This a new idea for me. (*Gesamtschule*)

> I don't think I can see yet what it really means. (*Gymnasium*)

Those teachers in both groups who had a university degree in English, had originally chosen that subject because of their anglophilia or americophilia. For them, a lingua franca focus posed a threat of losing solid linguistic ground:

> Despite everything, I think we cannot completely do without accuracy. We must at least keep accuracy in mind as an objective. (*Gesamtschule*)

> I have a thoroughly multicultural class. And I have some Africans there. And, I mean, English is their language. But I maintain that 'other' should be pronounced with a [ð], not a [d]. (*Gesamtschule*)

These teachers were also afraid that ELF might imply the loss of meaningful and complex communication, that teaching and learning could turn trivial and superficial.

> I think there is some danger that communication becomes extremely simplified and that something gets lost which one thought important. And if we want to teach English as a main subject, we must allow our teaching to reach some depth below the level of pure communication. To be honest, I have no idea how to tackle that. (*Gesamtschule*)

> Opening their minds to a lingua franca approach also means that you want to open their minds to encounters with a variety of cultures. But if you have a little bit of Chinese here and a little bit of Indian there, I feel the danger of superficiality. (*Gymnasium*)

> All this might turn out to be rather too wishy-washy. (*Gymnasium*)

Views from the Gymnasium staff

Although the above statements show that the two staff groups shared some basic common ground, the *Gymnasium* staff relied much more heavily on the maintenance of a cultural focus than the *Gesamtschule* teachers. They argued that there was no need to sacrifice Britain and the USA as main target cultures for the sake of lingua franca. In the long run, lingua franca competence would take care of itself. It would emerge as a by-product of a culture-specific approach, as long as that approach was sensitive to the inner plurality of the culture in question.

They argued for a continuity between traditional English teaching and the teaching of ELF and were convinced that the awareness of cultural relativity obtained in a culture-specific English language classroom would result in a general attitude of intercultural sensitivity useful in *lingua franca* situations. The second and third of the following comments broadened this argument by emphasising the fact that different target cultures were already inherent in English teaching.

> Language, literature and culture somehow belong together. When I learn a language, I begin by focusing on the cultural heritage that goes with that country, including modern developments. What I believe to be especially important is not so much that you integrate all cultures, but that you teach your students what we regard as cultural awareness, i.e. that we are open for everything else. But for me, a language is always interlinked with a culture. When I learn Russian, I deal with Russian culture. And when I learn French, I deal with French culture.

> You need not limit yourself to Great Britain and Australia. Our textbooks also give us some ideas on how to include Indian or African cultures and the post-colonial period... If you put too much stress on the lingua franca thing, everything becomes the same. Yes, I feel that nowadays so many things are already the same everywhere, through globalisation. And now the same applies to cultures. You would have to generalise, and in order to generalise, you must give up the typical, the unique. I must admit that would make me feel sorry.

> The special thing about English is that we already have to open up our perspective from England to the USA, to Australia, and so on. So we know that conventions in England may be unacceptable even in the USA.

One member of the staff regarded the interplay between culture-specific English language teaching inside the classroom and ELF outside the classroom as a promising road to the complex English competence required today.

> I wouldn't go so far as to make a concept of lingua franca. Because what you really have is two different objectives that fit together excellently. Our students often gain their motivation for English from their experience outside school, and they know that what they learn is also a lingua franca. What they expect from us, at school, is cultural knowledge. They want information about the specific countries. Everything else must be left to real life.

These teachers felt that a good command of standard British English was far from being an impediment in a lingua franca situation as long as the speakers were aware of the difficulties of negotiating meaning with speakers from other backgrounds. The students in their *Gymnasium* were given the chance of developing that awareness in an exchange programme with a Swedish partner school in which English served as a means of communication and in occasional multinational projects with English as the link language.

There was one area, however, in which that staff felt more had to be done – pronunciation. Although their textbooks were accompanied by cassettes with different speakers of English – Indian, Pakistani, Geordie, Nigerian etc. – the students found it hard to tolerate non-standard pronunciation in real life: 'Whenever our French exchange students visit', the teachers explained to me, 'they join our English classes, too. Their pronunciation has a lot of entertainment value for our students, so much so that they do not pay attention to *what* the French students say because they are too amused about *how* they say it.'

To sum up the findings from this school:

- ELF was regarded as basically a by-product of an Anglo-American focus in English teaching, on condition that the approach was not overly monocultural.
- The teachers considered ELF as a less interesting approach as compared to traditional English teaching because they assumed it to be cultureless and somehow neutral, empty and abstract.
- Linguistically, the BrE or, to a lesser degree, AmE standards were maintained.
- In the realm of accent, teachers planned to broaden their pupils' experience in dealing with different types of pronunciation.

Views from the Gesamtschule staff

For some of the *Gesamtschule* teachers, the impending loss of a national-native culture in the English language classroom was regarded as a potential gain for their students. During in-service training, these teachers had been advised to create an English atmosphere for their lessons, but had been reluctant to take up the advice because they knew that it was beside the point for their pupils who would probably never travel to England. They had, however, established an exchange programme with US-American partners in which successful students took part. But the majority, these teachers felt, would rarely get in touch with the 'inner circle' of native speakers of English.

> Our students are not likely to travel to England. Some travel to America, but that is a privilege. Turkey or Italy or maybe Mallorca are much more likely places for most of them and these are the places for which they may need some English.

Right at the beginning of the interview, one of the teachers admitted that the idea of a lingua franca, though rather new to her, took a burden off her shoulders. She was relieved, because the fact that she had not offered her classes the full British and American cultural programme had always made her feel guilty. ELF held the promise of more relevance and accessibility for her.

> If we start from the reality that we have here, if we start from the clientele we have here, then the lingua franca approach seems to me much more realistic. That is what the students will do with English… And as for myself, you know, this thought comes as a kind of relief to me, because in some of the forms some students really have a hard time struggling with what we want them to swallow. And – yes, I find this thought a relief.

This pragmatic and hopeful view was shared by one of her colleagues who was also troubled by the gap between English textbook topics and the world of his students.

Whenever I take a student's perspective I simply cannot understand why he should study a text about the British Museum when he has never even seen a museum or a library in Hamburg from inside. This is totally beyond his sphere of interest.

While the grammar school teachers had maintained the need to keep up a native linguistic standard, these teachers – though also worried about the unknown – were on the whole more ready to discover new communicative ground. This did not keep them from seeking some kind of standard, but they approached the problem in an exploratory rather than a normative manner, with the issue of successful practical communication uppermost on their minds.

You know, it occurs to me that we would have to invent the language that we are supposed to teach.

How does a lingua franca function?

For me it's the following aspect that worries me: How can a lingua franca remain a lingua franca? There must be some common ground or it drifts apart just as the British and the American English has drifted apart and has reached a point where you communicate without understanding each other. How can a lingua franca contribute to mutual understanding?

To sum up the findings from the comprehensive school:

- Everything considered, most of these teachers were more at ease with the idea of a shift away from traditional school English, both linguistically and culturally.
- They were, however, also convinced that some form of common ground, some lingua franca standard, was necessary in order to allow for communicative interaction with speakers of other languages.

Although varying in degree, both discussions revealed some reservations about a loss of linguistic, territorial or cultural reference for their English teaching. The teachers were in search of a convincing answer to the question: What are we to teach? Whose English? Whose culture? These are fundamental questions at the heart of the overall lingua franca debate where they feature as the contentious issue of ownership. I shall discuss this issue within the wider framework of that debate before returning to the language classroom.

The Issue of Ownership in the Lingua Franca Debate

There is an interesting distinction that can be found in definitions of a lingua franca. For some, it is a means of communication between speakers of different mother tongues, including native speakers of the language used as lingua franca. Others are clearly restrictive and describe it as 'a medium of communication between people of different mother tongues for whom it is a second language' (Samarin, 1987, quoted in Gnutzmann, 2000: 26). In this radical opinion, native speakers are excluded from the lingua franca community. There is also, of course, a third position, that includes native speakers while making them newcomers to the lingua franca world in a different way:

Here, native speakers are seen as needing to adjust linguistically, socially, and culturally in international situations just as much as anyone else: speaking with care, avoiding unnecessary idioms and slang, and toning down their regionalisms... (McArthur, 1998: 24)

It may seem a little surprising that the role of native speakers should play such an important part in the lingua franca debate and that there should be views that go so far as to exclude them from the lingua franca community. The position becomes clear, however, if one considers that the dream of a common language has always been accompanied and sustained by visions of world democracy and universal equality. Such visions were infused with the conviction that no living national language could fulfil the demands of a truly democratic language for all. A national language as lingua franca would inevitably mean an unhealthy imbalance in favour of native speakers of that language and their economic, cultural and social practices. It would be imposed upon the world by means of money, guns and ideologies of supremacy. The whole idea of a lingua franca continues to be permeated by fears of economic and cultural domination and loss of language and identity. This deep-rooted anxiety explains the distrust of native speakers in lingua franca contexts. In the history of post-colonialism and post-communism it has given rise to frequent struggles and has sparked off many a separatist and liberation movement in places where linguae francae like Russian, Spanish, French, Hindi, English, but also more regional languages dominate the public sphere at the expense of native languages, reducing these to home languages.

The case of English is affected by that difficult background. The circumstances of its rise from a small western European island to a global means of communication seems to confirm the suspicions of thinkers like Comenius, Descartes, Leibniz and many others before and after them who were interested in a neutral world language.

The desire for neutrality has meant that powerful 'natural' languages cannot serve (in the eyes of the language makers) for they are tinged, as it were, by history and 'imperial prestige'. Thus the way has been seen as theoretically clear for a constructed language to fill a yawning and bothersome gap. (Edwards, 1994: 44)

For a variety of reasons, however, constructed languages never stood a chance (cf. Edwards, 1994: 43–7). For better, for worse – English has taken the place accorded to them. But the question of participation continues to be asked, now transformed into the question: Whose English?

Answers to that question again reveal two controversial positions. On the one hand, there are the supporters of standard British English as the educational norm, prominent amongst them John Honey. In *Language is Power* (1997: 246) he pleads for standard British English as the model for a lingua franca, because it stands for an impressive tradition and history and is 'the vehicle of great literature and the exponent of admired values'. He denies that it is a class dialect and argues that no society – whether national nor international – can function without an agreed linguistic standard.

On the other hand, there are educators like Marko Modiano who take up a more open view. In an article entitled 'Standard English(es) and educational practices for the world's *lingua franca'* (1999) he examines the future of language instruction and states that

> (t)raditionally, for European educational purposes, standard English has been considered by many to be standard British English (BrE) with RP pronunciation, and the goal of instruction has been the achievement of near-native proficiency based on this variety... Leading language experts in the UK, however, view standard English as being represented in two varieties, BrE and standard American English (AmE). If one perceives the language from an international point of view, it is apparent that these as well as other commonly held notions of language beg to be refuted. (Modiano, 1999: 3)

He regrets that definitions of standard are more often exclusive than inclusive and that they do not take non-native speakers into account. [Incidentally, the combination of Modiano's view in the lingua franca controversy and his Italian name led Tom McArthur to suspect him of 'the frustration of a competent non-native language professional' (1999: 4) before he found out that Modiano was an American born and bred.]

Like Honey, Modiano (1999: 4) does not approve of an abolition of standard, but he rejects 'a prescriptive model which is possessed by privileged native speakers of a "prestige" variety'. Instead he believes that

> from a global perspective, it is not apparent that British 'tradition'... is something admirable... A linguistic chauvinism, or if you will, ethnocentricity, is so deeply rooted, not only in British culture, but also in the minds and hearts of a large number of language teachers working abroad, that many of the people who embrace such bias find it difficult to accept that other varieties of English, for some learners, are better choices for the educational model in the teaching of English as a foreign or second language. (Modiano, 1999: 6f.)

In his search for a standard, Modiano does not look to some linguistic authority, but to 'the speech communities which currently claim the English language as their own'. He finds a discrepancy between written and spoken English, the former being relatively standardised internationally, the latter increasingly diversified around the world. It is the spoken English that he finds in need of standardisation.

> Standard English, as a spoken standard, must by definition only include forms of the language which are comprehensible to competent speakers of the language world-wide. Native speakers who speak with strong regional accents (and certainly dialects) are not, in my definition, speakers of Standard English... The designation 'standard English' should be rooted in the communicative value of language. (Modiano,1999: 7).

He illustrates his view as follows:

> English as an international language (EIL) illustrated as those features of English which are common to all native and non-native varieties. (Modiano, 1999: 10)

This is, of course, an abstract concept but it shows that a simple reference to a national concept of language and culture is insufficient. A lingua and cultura franca come into being if some common ground is created between speakers who are prepared to step out of their more monocultural or 'national' homes.

Looking back at the staff interviews, one could say with some simplification that the *Gymnasium* teachers shared some of Honey's views (though not his chauvinist stance). They felt that the communicative needs of their students were best served in encounters with the language of standard native speakers. In addition, school ought to provide occasions for listening to the voices of non-native speakers of English and to heighten the esteem for their unfamiliar pronunciation. Apart from that, the traditional target cultures at the centre of English language education were seen as too valuable to be given up.

The general attitude of the *Gesamtschule* staff, on the other hand, seemed to be closer to Modiano's. Most of these teachers took their students' future communicative needs as the point of departure for their teaching, and the idea of *lingua franca* seemed to allow for more of that. Encounters with standard speakers were not high on the agenda. Despite some uneasiness expressed about the uncertain linguistic foundation of ELF, it seemed to allow for a less normative, more process-oriented view of communication. The shift from sophistication towards successful negotiation of meaning promised to favour simplification. It seemed to give space for less instruction on the teachers' part and more exploring on the students' part.

Most of the staff would probably have agreed wholeheartedly with what Byram describes as John G. Christensen's view of less privileged learners:

> … their own cultural capital, even if not dominant in their own society, should be valued in any interaction, as is the cultural capital of their interlocutors. This is particularly important for those learners who do not have access to the dominant culture in their own or another society and who are therefore not attracted by the worlds which FLT offers them. (Byram, 2000: 14)

In comparison, the more socially ambitious context of the *Gesamtschule* as well as its multi-cultural and multi-lingual everyday reality seemed to be more compatible with the project of ELF than the more academically ambitious and linguistically homogeneous context of the grammar school.

Some Implications for Language Teaching and Teacher Education

What are the conclusions to be drawn for language teaching and teacher education? Does it follow from the aforesaid that English studies are an impediment to ELF; that the objective of near–nativeness blocks the way to ELF much as nativeness excludes speakers from the lingua franca community in Samarin's view (see above); does it follow that ELF is a pidgin for the educationally less privileged? These conclusions would certainly be naive and wrong. It must be borne in mind that the interviews centred around the *future* of English teaching. So far both groups still felt very much compelled to teach their classes 'proper English'; the difference between them lay in their assessment of that focus and their readiness to embrace it or to embark upon a modified approach. Whether the demands of an ELF approach are more or less difficult remains to be seen, and the question of student success depends on too many factors to be included here. At this point in time, all we can say is that ELF would mean a change of perspective. David Crystal writes:

> ... teachers need to prepare their students for a world of staggering linguistic diversity. Somehow, they need to expose them to as many varieties of English as possible, especially those which they are most likely to encounter in their own locale. And above all teachers need to develop a truly flexible attitude towards principles of usage. (Crystal, 1999: 17).

A vast and hybrid field opens up before teachers and students of English. In Crystal's words:

> the chief task facing English language teaching is how to devise pedagogical policies and practices in which the need to maintain an international standard of intelligibility, in both speech and writing, can be made to comfortably exist alongside the need to recognise the importance of international diversity, as a reflection of identity, chiefly in speech and eventually perhaps also in writing. (Crystal, 1999: 20)

English teacher education in Germany needs to take up this challenge. At present, that education remains very much embedded in the philological realm of British and American studies, both culturally and linguistically, with a literary canon that mirrors the 'Great Tradition'. It continues in the vein

> of the Herder-Humboldt notion that languages must be seen as expressions of cultures so that one's own language means the acculturation to one's own culture and foreign language learning the acculturation to a foreign culture. As far as languages are concerned, all pedagogical programmes since the mid-19th century have been based on that conviction. (Hüllen, 1998: 288, my translation)

For the dream of a common language to come true, this notion must be reconsidered.

Such a reconsideration is not limited to the subject of English. A while ago, a colleague of mine spoke about something he had observed during a visit to a primary school. He was waiting outside the staff room (which is firmly barred against outsiders, especially pupils, in most German schools), watching a little girl obviously waiting like him, but much more impatiently. Finally a teacher turned up and she flew towards him, eagerly crying in German: 'I've been waiting for you with four eyes'. Now, 'waiting with four eyes' is not a German metaphor. The child had evidently transferred it from her first language into her second. The question is what to make of it. Is such an instance an intrusion into the German language, leading to an intolerable language mix? Is the child guilty of usurpation? Or does the vivid new image conjure the situation of waiting so that it comes alive in an unexpected and forceful manner, drawing attention to the power of words, very much like poetry?

In Modiano's illustration of English as an international language he describes that language as a common core. The question of ownership has been resolved: It belongs to nobody, or rather to everyone who – using and sharing it – creates it. From this point of view, Peter Bichsel's (1997) dictum: 'There is just One Language', and his approval of Jean Paul's: 'Learning language is superior to learning languages', begin to make sense.

Notes

1. As a random example see *Lehrplan des Ministeriums für Bildung, Wissenschaft, Forschung und Kultur des Landes Schleswig-Holstein, Sekundarstufe I*: 'Englisch als wichtigste Weltsprache trägt in mittelnder Funktion dazu bei, in jungen Menschen Offenheit für kulturelle Vielfalt zu fördern, Verständnis für andere Völker zu entwickeln und Kenntnisse über historische, geographische, wirtschaftliche und politische Zusammenhänge zu erwerben. Damit fördert das Fach die Entfaltung der Persönlichkeit und hilft den Schülerinnen und Schülern, sich in der Welt zu orientieren. ... Die Öffnung des europäischen Binnenmarktes führt zu größerer Mobilität der Menschen und noch stärkerer Zusammenarbeit von Institutionen. Der Kenntnis des Englischen kommt angesichts dieser veränderten politischen Strukturen fundamentale Bedeutung für den einzelnen zu, indem es ihm die Übernahme von Verantwortung sowie den Aufbau internationaler Kontakt im öffentlichen Leben über Landesgrenzen hinweg eröffnet. Angesichts der Realität grenzüberschreitenderm Informationsmedien und Kommunikationsmöglichkeiten ermöglichen englische Sprachkenntnisse die direkte Nutzung von Informationen in englischer Sprache. Damit wird ein Beitrag geleistet zur Vorbereitung der Schülerinnen und Schüler auf ihre Stellung als Bürgerinnen und Bürger in Europa' (16f.)

   In a recent report commissioned by the Kultusministerkonferenz on the future of upper secondary schooling in Mathematics, German and English, the experts agreed on the view, 'dass das Fach Englisch in der gymnasialen Oberstufe auf Grund der lingua-franca-Funktion des Englischen einen anderen Status hat als die anderen (neuen und alten) Fremdsprachen. ... Aus dieser Perspektive wird vor allem die neuphilologische, an Literatur und Landeskunde orientierte Tradition des Englischunterrichts kritisiert. Sie ist für ein zeitgemäßes Kerncurriculum nicht mehr zu legitimieren' (Tenorth, 2001: 156, 157).

2. The guidelines for English studies at Hamburg University support the students' statements: 'Die Gegenstände des Faches umfassen die englische Sprache und ihre Varietäten, die Literaturen Großbritanniens und Nordamerikas, selektiv auch die des früheren Commonwealth sowie allgemein die Kulturen dieser verschiedenen englischsprachig-geographischen Bereiche. Das Fach Englisch kann in seiner Gesamtheit für das Studium der verschiedenen Lehrämter gewählt werden, mit der Möglichkeit der Schwerpunktbildung im britischen, amerikanischen oder linguistischen Bereich.' (http://www.sign-lang.uni-hamburg.de/fb07/Stuplan/EnglSprache.html)

Correspondence

Any correspondence should be directed to Dr Helene Decke-Cornill, Universität Hamburg, Fachbereich Erziehungswissenschaft, Von-Melle-Park 8, 20146 Hamburg, Germany (decke-cornill@erzwiss.uni-hamburg.de).

References

Bichsel, P. (1997) Es gibt nur Eine Sprache. *Praxis Deutsch* 144, 4–9.
Breidbach, S. (2002) European Communicative Integration: The function of foreign language teaching for the development of a European public sphere. *Language, Culture and Curriculum* 15 (3).
Byram, M. (2000) Learning language without a culture? The case of English as a *lingua franca*. In L. Bredella, F.-J. .Meißner, A. Nünning and D. Rösler (eds) *Wie ist Fremdverstehen lehr- und lernbar?* Tübingen: Gunter Narr.

Crystal, D. (1999) The future of Englishes. *English Today* 15 (2), 10–20.

Decke-Cornill, H. (1999) Einige Bedenken angesichts eines möglichen Aufbruchs des Fremdsprachenunterrichts in eine bilinguale Zukunft. *Neusprachliche Mitteilungen* 3, 164–170.

Decke-Cornill, H. (2001) Pluralität und sprachliche Bildung. In D. Abendroth-Timmer and G. Bach (eds) *Mehrsprachiges Europa* (pp. 177–189) Tübingen: Gunter Narr.

Edwards, J. (1994) *Multilingualism*. Harmondsworth: Penguin.

Flick, U. (1995) *Qualitative Forschung. Theorie, Methoden, Anwendung in Psychologie und Sozialwissenschaften*. Reinbek bei Hamburg: Rowohlt.

Gnutzmann, C. (2000) Englisch als globale *lingua franca*. In G. Henrici and E. Zöfgen (eds) *Fremdsprachen lehren und lernen*. Tübingen: Gunter Narr.

Honey, J. (1997) *Language is Power*. London: Faber.

Hüllen, W. (1987) *Englisch als Fremdsprache*. Tübingen: Francke.

Hüllen, W. (1998) ghoti – das Leittier der internationalen Kommunikation oder: Das Englische als National- und als Weltsprache. In I. Gogolin, G. List and S. Graap (eds) *Über Mehrsprachigkeit*. Tübingen: Stauffenburg.

McArthur, T. (1998) Guides to tomorrow's English. *English Today* 14 (3), 21–26.

McArthur, T. (1999) Relevance and resonance? – An editorial aside. *English Today* 15 (4), 4.

Ministerium für Bildung, Wissenschaft, Forschung und Kultur des Landes Schleswig-Holstein (1997) *Lehrplan für die Sekundarstufe I der weiterführenden allgemeinbildenden Schulen – Hauptschule, Realschule, Gymnasium, Gesamtschule – Englisch*. Kiel.

Mondiano, M. (1999) Standard English(es) and educational practices for the world's *lingua franca*. *English Today* 15 (4), 3–13.

'Stellungnahmen: Englisch ab der 1. Klasse'. *Die Woche* 17, April 21, 2000.

Tenorth, H.-E. (2001) *Kerncurriculum Oberstufe. Mathematik – Deutsch – Englisch*. Weinheim und Basel: Beltz.

Teaching India in the EFL-Classroom: A Cultural or an Intercultural Approach?

Reinhold Wandel
Otto-von-Guericke Universität, IFPH, Postfach 4120, 39016 Magdeburg, Germany

The concept of English as a world language implies that the focus of English teaching should not only be on the traditional countries and cultures such as Britain and the United States. Simultaneously, English teaching should also develop learners' intercultural sensitivity. The choice of India as a focus for English teaching provides both a wider range of interest and also the means for developing awareness of cultural diversity. The latter, however, requires not just cognitive but also affective engagement with teaching materials, and many textbooks have not yet achieved the means to develop both. This article provides a critical analysis of textbooks in Germany that are beginning to offer new approaches.

Teaching English as a World Language

Taking the reality of English as a 'world language' seriously, EFL-teaching must enhance its geographical scope and include non-mainstream cultures. Thus areas/countries, so far neglected, will play an increasingly more relevant role. On the other hand, educating students to make use of English as a lingua franca also means to accustom them to being interculturally sensitive. In this context we have to decide whether we should focus on teaching national target cultures or whether an intercultural approach should be applied in which general cultural patterns and structures are introduced.

This potentially controversial issue is exemplified by a discussion of how India has been and can be presented to an EFL-audience. Traditionally India found her way into the EFL-scene by means of her role as 'the jewel in the crown'. From about 1980 onwards the growing interest in multicultural Britain led to a presentation of the Indian minority (in Britain). It is a fairly recent phenomenon that EFL-teaching realised that the way to India did not need a detour via Britain, but that there was a direct link to the English language within the context of the Indian subcontinent and its cultures.

So far, textbooks etc. have provided hardly any material for teachers and students who want to take up India in the classroom. When analysing some rare chapters on India in recent German anthologies, it becomes obvious that sociocultural problems are emphasised in a cognitive-orientated and detached way. Of course, knowledge about and a socio-critical view on the target culture is essential. But rather than providing information, when teaching adolescents it is more important to apply an approach supporting the affective level of learning, to select teaching material that contains and reflects the experience of the students' peer-group and, above all, to use a contrastive perspective so that 'the other' is closely linked and compared with one's own background.

It is estimated that within 10 years the number of people using and communicating in English as a second or foreign language will be considerably higher than the number of native speakers (Crystal, 1997: 130). Thus, English is essential as the global language, as a functional tool for cross-cultural communication in international settings, in transport, tourism, conferences, for surfing the internet, for scientific research. In Germany our major science journals are now published in English, and some educationalists claim that the command of English is as fundamental a cultural technique as is reading and writing – and that this no longer applies only to the cultural, social and economic elites. Taking the idea and the reality of English as a 'world lingua franca' seriously, EFL-teaching (in Germany, in Europe – and elsewhere) will be confronted with a change of paradigms, and this trend will imply changes of perspectives in the content and organisation of language teaching (and it will also change the way teachers of English are educated). In Germany, for example, the relevance of world-wide English has led to a reconsideration as to when schoolchildren should start learning English, and the introduction of 'early English', as it is called, is now one of the major shifts in the German educational system, i.e. children will start learning English at the age of eight or even six – nation-wide.

The old notion of teaching English in non-native surroundings (such as in Germany) is to provide our young people with the proper linguistic skills to communicate with somebody who is a native speaker, i.e. with a Briton or an American. In secondary school textbooks pupils are introduced to an English (not British) family, living in Hatfield, Nottingham or Chester; they learn about family life, the parents' jobs, their shopping habits, the school life of their relevant 'peer-group'. The textbook characters meet friends or go out for a meal in a snack bar or restaurant. On holiday, the children travel to the seaside or visit an aunt in Wales or Scotland; the school organises a trip to London, and Scotland or London are thus included as topics or teaching units, and so on. After three years the textbooks switch to the United States and usually for two further years relevant aspects of American society are portrayed – in accordance with the increased maturity of the pupils. Thus EFL-learners in Germany are – as a rule – only confronted with the target cultures of the US or the UK. (It should be added, however, that textbooks for learners in the sixth year often include one chapter on Australia.)

However, if we consider the role of English as a world language, two major shifts regarding the cultural dimension of our educational work seem unavoidable:

(1) EFL-teaching must enhance its cultural and geographical scope and include other English-speaking cultures apart from the UK and the USA. Thus areas/countries such as South Africa, Nigeria, Australia, Canada, India and their cultural backgrounds must be taken into consideration and will start playing an increasingly more relevant role in the EFL-classroom.

(2) On the other hand, educating students to make use of English as a lingua franca also means developing their intercultural sensitivity. Students should be allowed to get to know a number of different cultural outlooks and perspectives. They ought to be provided with tools to analyse fundamental aspects of cultures.

Textbooks should contain material that allows and provokes diverging opinions and discussions on cultural stereotyping. At the same time, some attitudes and behaviours should be developed: the feeling of empathy, the ability to change perspectives, to recognise (the reasons for) misunderstandings and to find ways to overcome them. Students should be given communicative and pragmatic tools to 'negotiate meaning', to develop interactive and meta-linguistic skills, to be able to tolerate and endure ambiguity. Generally, 'FLT should… concentrate on equipping learners with the means of accessing and analysing any cultural practices and meanings they encounter…' (Byram, 2000: 15).

Thus, in this context it is crucial to decide whether the focus of cultural aspects in EFL-teaching should aim at specific national or regional target cultures (which often are quite alien to the European/Western background and need to be explained and illustrated) or whether an intercultural approach should be applied in which general cultural patterns and structures are introduced and unfamiliar concepts are compared to the cultural environment of the students. This potentially controversial issue will be exemplified by outlining and discussing how India (and her cultures) has been and can be presented to a German/European EFL-audience.

India Perceived as Part of Britain

Traditionally India found her way into the German EFL-scene by means of her role as 'the jewel in the crown', as part of the British empire. In the true Arnoldian spirit, which in German grammar schools was practised under the name of 'Kulturkunde', aesthetically outstanding thoughts and writings were selected; thus, for example, short stories by Kipling or Forster's *Passage to India* and – more recently – Ruth Prawer Jhabvala's *Heat and Dust* were read with advanced students. Yet the reality of colonial or postcolonial India was only taken into account in order to provide some background information that was needed for the students to understand the literary texts. Generally, this philological and eurocentric perspective focused on the British in India, or, to be more explicit, on British 'high' literature set in colonial India.

The 1970s saw the beginning of a new direction in the field of cultural studies within foreign language teaching. The social, cultural and economic realities of the countries concerned were no longer omitted or avoided. The idea of eternal cultural values and the belief in a 'harmonious nation under God', that were predominant in the teaching of 'Landeskunde' in non-political post-war West Germany, were replaced by the critical realisation that, as far as Britain was concerned, the population was not confined to the middle- and upper-class bounds of the home counties. Based on redefinitions of the concept of culture (cf. Raymond Williams, Richard Hoggart or the CCCS in Birmingham) different notions and 'ways of life' were discovered, for example working-class life in the North of England, and so were class conflicts or youth culture or the conflict in Northern Ireland or minorities, or even the fact that Welsh is still spoken in parts of Wales and that this is a highly sensitive and political issue. (As for the US, there suddenly emerged – saved from the loss of memory and from utter negligence – highly interesting findings such as the fact that there existed black people and Red Indians, i.e. native Americans, and that the American dream does not always come true.)

It is in this context that from about 1980 onwards the growing interest in multicultural Britain led to another approach towards India and South Asians. Now the Indian minority in Britain – their problems regarding integration, employment, racial abuse, etc. – turned up as a topic in textbooks and annotated readers. Cornelsen's *English G C 3*, for example, featured a report headlined 'Racists use fire to threaten family'. Faruk Dhondy's short stories were a source of inspiration for 'avant-garde' teachers; moreover, the German publishing houses leading in the field of language teaching edited simplified narratives such as the story *Shemaz* in which the conflicts between father and daughter within a Pakistani family were portrayed and which is quite widely read in German classrooms today. And in the latest set of textbooks for English used in German schools, Sarah and Debbie, John and Nick as typical English kids are accompanied by schoolmates named Sanjay and Sita whose parents run an Indian restaurant in Chester. From the British in India the perspective has changed to the Indians in Britain. In both cases, however, the focus of EFL-teaching is aimed at coming to grips with what may be called British national culture, of which the 'Indian dimension' is just a regional, social or historical subcategory.

India Perceived in Her Own Right

It is, indeed, a fairly recent phenomenon that German EFL-teaching started to realise that the way to India did not need a detour via Britain and the British, but that there was a direct link to the English language and to English language speakers (as well as to literary texts using English) within the context of the Indian subcontinent and its cultures. This delayed socio-political insight is not really surprising. Researching the role of the Third World in German textbooks for English, Kubanek found that non-European areas and cultures are not really represented and the Third World does not appear as an independent topic to be dealt with for its own sake (Kubanek, 1987: 3).

Kubanek's investigation dates from about 1985, and within the last decade there has been some geopolitical change. The 'global village' has widened our views, and critical concepts and theories such as orientalism, decolonisation, postcolonialism and resistance to eurocentricity have led to the fact that a minority of German EFL-teachers have started to question the emphasis on the established mainstream cultures, and areas and topics that used to be marginalised or did not really exist are now being considered worthy of integration into the syllabus. Recent revisions of English curricula in Northrhine-Westfalia, Brandenburg or Saxony-Anhalt explicitly request the treatment of postcolonial countries and themes. In this way Indians in South Asia, still quite timidly, but step by step, start appearing in some textbooks. In *Notting Hill Gate 4 B* the love story between Shah Jahan and Mumtaz-i-Mahal – and, of course, the Taj Mahal itself – are presented, whereas *English Live 5 B* describes life in a village in Tamil Nadu.

These are still exceptions, however. So far, textbooks, anthologies, readers, etc. have provided hardly any material for teachers and students who want to take up the topic of India in the classroom. Whereas for *Abitur* students (i.e. those studying for the examination at the end of upper secondary education) the internet is open to collect information, and newspapers, short stories and novels can be made use of, teaching India to younger students does not really happen, since the teachers committed to this task and in search of suitable material are offered no help.

The value of India as a topic

India is a relevant topic within the EFL-classroom. It is a huge subcontinent with almost a billion people, competing with China as the world's most populated country. It is the biggest democracy in the world and has established itself as a nuclear power. There is an Indian-style software Silicon Valley, in Bangalore. However, it is known to be a very poor country with a high rate of illiteracy in backward regions. English as a second or foreign language might be spoken by about 100 million people. It is used as the link-language for many inter-state negotiations, for administration, commerce, tourism, for the law and by the military personnel. And, last but not least, there are a number of eminent Indian writers expressing themselves in the English language; novels by authors such as Rushdie or Vikram Seth have acquired world fame.

When we get involved in teaching 'India in the EFL-classroom', some fundamental issues must be raised and some general decisions must be taken. Which stereotypes have to be overcome? Which 'aspects' of India should be taken into account? When presenting India (in textbooks, in anthologies, in the classroom), which features should be emphasised? What should be neglected – or omitted? Does teaching (about) India mean to increase the students' knowledge about facts and figures on South Asia or does it imply making them aware of their own cultural self-centredness (when being confronted with something strange and unusual)?

As for Germany, the negative stereotyping of India is problematic and needs to be questioned. Summing up a survey on how India is portrayed in the German media, Linkenbach-Fuchs concludes: 'India almost only seems to appear if something negative has to be proven' (1998: 52, my translation).

Looking at and analysing the way India is presented in two widely used anthologies and textbooks for upper-secondary students, we find carefully and sensibly selected materials and topics. *Top Line's* Chapter 2 ('India') (1992) for example contains the following texts:

- The Raj through Indian eyes.
- The poorest country in the world (Naipaul).
- Gandhi's Salt March.
- Midnight, 14 August 1947.
- The practical process of partitioning (excerpt from Shashi Tharoor: *The Great Indian Novel.*)
- Souls crying out for God (Prawer Jhabvala).
- Freedom and suppression (Anita Desai).
- The grim face of the caste system.
- Life in a Bombay shanty-town.
- A country of extremes: Peasants waiting for rain // Monsoon (poems).
- Superpower rising.

Panorama (English cultures around the world), published in 1986, in Chapter 9 ('Post-independent India – Tradition and transition') presents the following items:

- Changes in traditional values.
- Underdevelopment and its causes.
- Back to the village.

- The Tractor and the Corn Goddess (short story by Anand).
- Family planning and family welfare.
- Three short texts on 'English in India'.
- Discrimination: a case study.
- The scourge of Untouchability.
- Harijans and Hindu society: new problems.
- Dr Ambedkar – pioneer of human rights.

These rare chapters and units on India emphasise the social and cultural problems within Indian society in an honest and convincing way. Taking up topics such as the caste system, poverty, the role of Gandhi, the position of women, etc. the editors of these compilations offer a critical survey featuring the essential present-day socio-economic problems of India.

Certainly, one could argue that urban middle-class life is not really an issue here, that the diversity of Indian cultures has not really been presented and that too much stress may have been laid on poverty; but, on the other hand, Dalits are not only mentioned as passive and destined to remain within the lowest strata of society, but in the case of Dr Ambedkar they are shown in their resistance against exploitation and suppression. One could conclude that the editors have chosen a fair, an interesting and motivating set of ideas and stimuli for discussion. Having studied these authentic texts and having become acquainted with the important and relevant information here, German EFL-students, it is hoped, should have acquired some insight into the social reality and problems of contemporary India.

Thus, along the conventional line of EFL-teaching a national Indian culture is presented. The geographic and cultural setting of Britain or Australia has been replaced by that of the South Asian subcontinent. However, tasks and questions put to the students to deal with the texts about India remain solely on the cognitive, intellectually argumentative level. To give some examples: 'Analyse symptoms and reasons for the decline of the Indian economy during the colonial period' (Buttjes, 1986b: 111). 'How would you explain the continued existence of untouchability? (Buttjes, 1986: 115); 'Describe Dr Ambedkar's career as a representative of the "depressed classes"' (Buttjes, 1986: 116). And some quotes from *Top Line* (Bülow *et al.*, 1992): 'What is the main theme of this text and how does the author deal with this subject?' (p. 38); 'What image of Gandhi do you get from the text?' (p. 42); 'Describe the process of partitioning India...' (p. 46). Texts and tasks supporting literature, imagination or a subjective and personal evaluation are hardly to be found.

This emphasis on detached issues and problems, this sociocultural approach is based on the post-1968 assumption that a socio-critical, non-affirmative view on India (or any other cultural sphere) will certainly convince young people that it is worth while studying and getting personally involved with this topic. But this pedagogical method of selecting and presenting mainly factual and informative texts to be summarised, discussed and critically evaluated in the classroom is not enough. There has been no attempt in the textbooks to prepare the students and raise their sensitivity by using pre-reading activities, by starting from the students' point of view, by finding ways of getting her or him into the mood to approach the given topic. Stereotypes, that have had such a devastating negative influence on the German concept of India, are not explicitly taken up, and there are no bridges offered to close the relatively wide cultural gap between the home and the target cultures. This analysis and critique can be generalised and applied to almost all readers and anthologies covering the dimensions of global English that are easily available for German EFL-teachers.

New Approaches to Teaching about India

Of course, 'the study of a country's culture rests to some extent on knowledge of its history and traditions' (Collie & Martin, 2000: 4), and we may add 'on knowledge of social contexts and social interaction, too'. But there is more to it than knowledge. In his analysis of 'Intercultural Management' the German economist Brandenburger has analysed and evaluated altogether 53 concepts and programmes of companies in which personnel for international management tasks – 'one world managers' – are selected and trained. One of the conclusions of his research lies in the warning not to neglect the affective dimensions when people are educated and prepared to cope with strange cultures. Only then, he states, does 'the psyche' get involved (Brandenburger, 1995: 92), and that is necessary to develop empathy, tolerance, flexibility, open-mindedness, curiosity, etc.

The focus on the target culture, as exemplified in the two textbooks that have been discussed, applies too much concern for the cognitive and lacks intercultural sensitivity. Facts and figures, cultural problems and social issues must be accompanied by an approach supporting the affective level of learning. It is in this context, moreover, that the use of fictional and imaginative texts is highly relevant, because they get the reader involved and, at the same time, are open for anticipation, speculation and diverging interpretations. The subjective, individualised and emotional character of literature supports not only strategies by which the reader may identify with the fictional world and its protagonists, but also encourages aspects that are of vital importance for intercultural understanding such as empathy and change of perspective (cf. Bredella, 2000; Nünning, 2000).

Apart from emphasising the affective dimension, teaching culture to adolescents must also imply that the material and the relevant aspects presented are selected in such a way that they contain and reflect the experience of the students' peer-group. For teenagers the target culture must lose its state of detachment, and it is by looking at the way their Indian counterparts behave and feel, what they appreciate and how they cope with family, school, spare time, hobbies and media, that genuine interest is elicited. Such an attitude and such a motivation will form a solid base for further exploration into unfamiliar cultural and social patterns.

Realising that young people in India share parts of the global youth culture, but that, on the other hand, some features – such as Bollywood movies, Indiapop, dating and courting – are intrinsically Indian and hard to grasp, European youngsters learn how to differentiate between various cultural concepts and realities. It is crucial to apply such a contrastive perspective so that 'the other' is closely linked and compared with their own background. 'Learners need to reflect on their own social identities and their own cultures in order to better understand those of other people...' (Byram, 2000: 15).

Unterricht Englisch (2001), one of the leading ELT-journals in Germany, attempted to apply these considerations to a more affective and contrastive presentation of the reality of the Indian subcontinent. For example, in the text 'How Sita and Deepak met' (cf. Pandurang, 2001) a Bombayite expert tries to explain the strange custom of 'arranged marriages' to German school students. Her careful and sensitive method is based on her experience with German students as a guest lecturer at Magdeburg University. She presents an individual case, evokes fears and hopes, but also explains the underlying habits and attitudes. Since the author knows both cultures, she can act as a mediator, and by means of diligence and caution, by continuous references to the German tradition students are gradually provided with the chance to comprehend and even to identify with the Indian way of finding a spouse: She repeatedly takes into account that the Indian customs might be strange for the German students, but since the German adolescents are engaged in their very own situation, they don't shrink back and don't refuse to get involved, ridiculing and despising those 'outdated conventions from far-off countries' – and soon losing interest; they become curious about this lonely hearts' club – by the permanent attempt to make them contrast their own mating and dating structures with those of their Indian peer-group. They are, for example, not only asked to find and analyse matrimonials in the internet, but also to write adverts as if they were looking for a partner for themselves, and by comparing these different ways of attracting a partner, the various virtues and predilections stated in the adverts, the diverging systems of social and emotional interaction become obvious and comprehensible.

In this same issue on India a collection of texts and tasks offered to the teacher for immediate use in the classroom includes an article about 'kissing', which is not done in public in India – again explained to German pupils by an Indian fellow student. Another page features an 'agony aunt' in Indian style, and a further text taken from an Indian teenage magazine presents suggestions for young people as to how they can design and decorate their rooms. Again, the German EFL-audience is asked to contribute to this design and to evaluate it (and to compare it with their own predilections).

It might be argued that in the examples given here the vital social and cultural problems of modern India are neglected, but the question must be posed why the majority of German or Swiss or French teenagers should show proper and intrinsic interest in Third World countries at all. Despite the www and CNN and the BBC World Service, India or South Africa are far away from the day-to-day experience for most of the European teenage population. In my opinion, by offering the facets of teenage life of the Indian peer-group as shown above, by contrasting these phenomena and attitudes with one's own and by emphasising a more affective approach, the danger of 'utter otherness' can be overcome and a closer relationship between the target culture and the EFL-student can be established. It is in this way and using this kind of procedures that interculturality can be enhanced and the focus on the specific national culture/s of India is not restricted to providing information, but serves as an example of how general cultural concepts can be accessed and intercultural learning can proceed.

Correspondence

Any correspondence should be directed to Dr Reinhold Wandel, Otto-von-Guericke-Universität, IFPH, Postfach 4120, 39016 Magdeburg, Germany (wandel-berlin@t-online.de).

References

Brandenburger, M. (1995) *Interkulturelles Management.* Köln: Botermann & Botermann.
Bredella, L. (2000) Fremdverstehen mit literarischen Texten. In L. Bredella, F.-J. Meißner, A. Nünning, and D. Rösler (eds) *Wie ist Fremdverstehen lehr-und lernbar?* (pp. 133–63). Tübingen: Gunter Narr.
Bülow, F.M. *et al.* (eds) (1992) *Top Line.* Stuttgart: Klett.
Buttjes, D. (1986a) *Panorama – English Cultures Around the World.* Dortmund: Lensing.
Buttjes, D. (1986b) *Panorama – Lehrerbuch.* Dortmund: Lensing.
Byram, M. (2000) Learning language without a culture? The case of English as a *lingua franca.* In L. Bredella *et al.* (eds) *Wie ist Fremdverstehen lehr– und lernbar?* (pp. 1–17). Tübingen: Gunter Narr.
Collie, J. and Martin, A. (2000) *What's It Like? Life and Culture in Britain Today. Teacher's Book.* Cambridge: Cambridge University Press.
Crystal, D. (1997) *English as a Global Language.* Cambridge: Cambridge University Press.
Kubanek, A. (1987) *Dritte Welt im Englischlehrbuch der Bundesrepublik Deutschland.* Regensburg: Friedrich Pustet.
Linkenbach-Fuchs, A. (1998) Realisiert sich eine Utopie? – Oder: Was sich in der Darstellung Indiens unbedingt ändern muß. In Landeszentrale für politische Bildung Baden-Württemberg (eds) *Revision des Indienbildes im Schulunterricht.* Stuttgart.
Nünning, A. (2000) 'Intermisunderstanding' – Prolegomena zu einer literaturdidaktischen Theorie des Fremdverstehens. In L. Bredella, F.-J. Meißner, A. Nünning and D. Rösler (eds) *Wie ist Fremdverstehen lehr-und lernbar?* (pp. 84–132). Tübingen: Gunter Narr.
Orton, E. (1996) *Shemaz.* Stuttgart: Klett.
Pandurang, M. (2001) How Sita and Deepak met. *Unterricht Englisch* 50, 41–6.

European Communicative Integration: The Function of Foreign Language Teaching for the Development of a European Public Sphere

Stephan Breidbach
Universität Bremen, Fachbereich 10, Postfach 330440, 28334 Bremen, Germany

The paradox of support for diversity and the drive for integration is one that is evident in the development of nation states and in the emergence of a new European space. The role played by language teaching in both historical phases is one that has to accept this general paradox, and in particular the relationship between language and identity. At a European level the wide use of English points towards increasing linguistic unity whereas multilingual education is promoted to support diversity. It is argued here that competence in English and complex, plurilingual competence are cornerstones for further European integration and the development of a European identity. A model of democratic participation dependent on diverse linguistic competences at different levels of democracy would provide the basis for communicative integration which is fundamental to the European project.

Linguistic Diversity and European Citizenship

The integration paradox: Unity in diversity

In the field of language politics, educators and politicians agree that European integration needs linguistic diversity to succeed. The national languages of the member states and the many regional languages within the EU need to play – as they actually do for many individuals in many contexts – an active role in people's lives. Any form of linguistic dominance through other languages or negligence of one's own language is regarded as a serious obstruction of the path towards integration. The general argument follows the line that languages express cultures and hence, cultural and linguistic diversity form a cornerstone of a European identity. Thus, the European Commission (1995: 47) writes:

> Languages are also the key to knowing other people. Proficiency in languages helps to build up the feeling of being European with all its cultural wealth and diversity and of understanding between the citizens of Europe... Multilingualism is part and parcel of both European identity/citizenship and the learning society.

The informing idea of this statement is a paradoxical one as it emphasises two antagonising concepts: comprehension of what is diverse and different, and the development of an integrated identity as a European citizen. This is, however, not at all inconsistent with the European history of ideas, which, as Bifulco points out, has been characterised by paradox since the beginning of modernity:

> Modern Europe proved to be a paradox right from the start. Its mission to civilise all of humanity coincided with the disappearance of medieval religious unity and, with the beginning of the age of great nations, of the dream

of political unity. These are contradictions we still live with today with the dawning of the opposite, albeit not incompatible, scenarios of globalisation and fragmentation (Bifulco, 1998: 4).

It might therefore be helpful, when analysing the process of European integration, to be prepared to accept paradox as one unifying factor: politically, it highlights the volatility of opinion and consensus within a process of constant re-establishing and re-construction. In fact, the institutionalisation of permanent political strife, channelled and contained within communicative processes of parliamentarianism and public opinion, can perhaps be seen as one of Europe's greatest cultural contributions to modern democracy. The reconciliation of opposing movements, unity and diversity, is at the core of European identity. One should expect to find these structures again when probing a little deeper into the function of language(s) and linguistic diversity.

In this paper, I wish to argue that the integration paradox is also at work in the field of language policy and foreign language education. While the widespread use of English points towards increasing linguistic unity, multilingual education is considered necessary to preserve cultural diversity. The development of a common, yet diverse, European identity hinges on whether both tendencies can be acknowledged in a constructive way. For a European public sphere, cultural literacy and the individual citizen's ability to enter processes of political and cultural deliberation are crucial aspects to give legitimacy to political decisions. With present and future communicative needs overarching many national and regional speech communities, I believe that both a high competence in English and a wide-ranging foreign language competence are cornerstones to further integration in Europe and to develop what is described as a European identity.

Politics of inclusion and exclusion through language in the process of formation of nation states

The context of unity and diversity, especially the development of the nation states in Europe, has always been closely tied to the question of a common, national language (cf. Barbour & Carmichael, 2000). As a consequence, language choice and the teaching of language(s) in state-controlled education became the subject of pedagogical, and equally political, controversy. At a very early stage, state authorities made a point of drawing a line between the national language as the language of general tuition, and foreign languages for which special language curricula were developed. In the late 18th century, the works of Johann Gottlieb Herder and Wilhelm von Humboldt became the intellectual source to link language with cultural identity, which again was seen as the well-spring for national identity. For my present purpose, I do not wish to discuss the conceptual differences between national and cultural identity. I am, however, well aware that they exist and the concepts should not be confused (for various theoretical frameworks cf. Hutchinson, 1987; Hutchinson & Smith, 1994; Oommen, 1997; Paulston, 1994).

By the end of the 19th century, school reformers, for example in Germany, explicitly aimed at linking language and national identity. They took a naturalistic view of the cultural within language, which, politically, left the study of foreign languages to highlight the intrinsic value – if not downright superiority –

of the German 'nature' as opposed to the Roman, and Anglo-Saxon 'nature' (cf. Albisetti, 1993: 193 ff.). One of the long-term effects of monocultural and monolingual nation-building is the widespread assumption even among today's foreign-language teachers that the prototypical European language learner is 'naturally' monolingual (cf. Gogolin, 1994). Another long-term effect originating here is the general conviction that languages are more or less immediate, perhaps exclusive and, in any case, unique manifestations of national or regional cultures.

This conviction gains political virulence and a potential for mobilisation as in contemporary times the ground for political inclusion has begun to shift. To provide inclusion and to give a sense of exclusiveness were the two equally important social functions in the formation of national citizenship in the countries of Europe, and language served for both:

> This national closure of citizenship was achieved, on the one hand, by the extension of rights and benefits to different strata of the civil society; on the other, by attributing some distinctiveness – 'shared' values, language, blood, history or culture – to the collective citizenry. The first of these acts transformed previously excluded populations into citizens, whereas the second ensured the exclusivity in membership. (Soysal, 1996: 17)

Soysal goes on to argue that after World War II 'the two major components of citizenship – identity and rights – are increasingly decoupled' (Soysal, 1996: 18). If this description of post-modern Europe is correct, Hutchinson's (1994) differentiation between political and cultural nationalism can help to understand that, in a situation in which the decision-making functions of the national states are increasingly both centralised to the level of the European Union and de-centralised to the level of the regions, language will retain its dominant position within the discourse of identity as one prime provider of cultural identity (cf. Schlesinger, 1994: 317). For the cultural nationalist, Hutchinson writes,

> [n]ations are… not just political units but *organic* beings, living personalities whose individuality must be cherished by their members in all their manifestations. Unlike the political nationalist, the cultural nationalist founds the nation not on 'mere' consent or law but on the passions implanted by nature or history. (Hutchinson, 1994: 122)

European Identity and Foreign Language Learning

Seen against this backdrop, Seeler (1997: 12–13) reformulates the European paradox in stating that cultural and linguistic diversity have to be preserved at the same time as citizens need to be enabled to communicate among themselves. If the history of Modern Europe highlights the triangular relationship between the existence of a national language, national identity, and the sovereign nation state, one ought to be sensitive to the potential of political power implied in any choice of one common language (p. 13). Still, Arntz (1998: 68) underlines the need for such a choice to be made within the very near future, even though this would mean the identification of a few 'privileged' languages as official languages. I believe that no prophetical talent is needed to state that English is very likely to evolve into one such – if not the only – lingua franca in Europe. Very strong pragmatic reasons speak in favour of this view. Firstly, from a quantitative point of view, English is the most widely taught foreign language in Europe. According to a Eurostat survey (Eurostat 53, 2001), English is taught to more than 90% of Europe's lower secondary pupils. Secondly, the virtual absence of a debate within the general public about this language choice works in favour of English as the dominant foreign language. There is certainly an ongoing debate among experts, with some contributions worthy of further debate. Nonetheless, the longer that no conscious and democratic decision is made, the more international communication will become impregnated with English. Arguably, the most urgent problems of our days are to be seen in a global and globalised context with English as the language of globalisation. Raasch (1999: 88) asks: 'Could it be that we really have an urgent need for such a world-encompassing language because the problems and phenomena are equally world-encompassing? In comparison, could regional languages even cope with this necessarily world-wide exchange?'

The role of English within a framework of multilingualism thus remains a complex one. However, the dominance of English makes it difficult to win learners over to the side of multilingualism, and to the extra effort to study another language (cf. Jeske, 2000; Vollmer, 2001), as they tend to consider proficiency in English as the most useful and prestigious, and thus sufficient, outcome of their foreign language studies. Judging from the results of another recent survey for the European Commission (Eurobarometer 54, 2001), this attitude seems indeed to be prevailing.

Within the last two and a half decades, supranational bodies such as the European Commission and the Council of Europe have taken political initiatives in the form of White Papers and Recommendations to promote individual multilingualism (Christ, 1998: 210). There are, however, differences as to how many and which languages should be learnt. The Commission paper considers it 'necessary for everyone… to acquire and keep up their ability to communicate in at least two Community languages in addition to their mother tongue' (European Commission, 1995: 47). The Commission implies, however, that the 'mother tongue' is a Community language too and thus its call for trilingual competence is restricted to Community languages. The Council of Europe takes a wider range of languages into view and encourages 'all Europeans to achieve a degree of communicative ability in a number of languages' (Council of Europe, 1998). On the whole, a number of pedagogical considerations are usually connected with these language learning concepts. They can be summarised as follows (cf. Christ, 1993; Meißner, 1998):

- promotion of life-long learning of foreign languages;
- access to languages of diverse linguistic families;
- awareness-raising to understand languages and multilingualism as a human asset;
- peaceful communication;
- learning languages as one aspect of intercultural learning.

In our historic situation, the study of English is intuitively plausible. If the result, however, is to be a *de facto* 'English-Only' situation in our schools, it will become difficult to meet the claim for linguistic diversity in Europe and the political and educational stances implied especially in the five aspects listed above. With reference to foreseeable concerns of democratic citizenship and social cohesion in Europe, I believe one other aspect needs to be brought to the foreground: the creation of and participation in a political space by European citizens. Inevitably, access to such a space of public discourse, in its most immediate sense, is given through languages.

European Integration and Democracy

At this point, I wish to return to the introductory idea that 'Europe has been structured around one idea: that idea is diversity and coping with diversity' (Schöpflin, 2000: 34). Schöpflin writes that soon there will be 'a threshold to be crossed':

> The next step in the integration of Europe – eastward enlargement – will give rise to problems as yet barely formulated, let alone clearly understood. Currently, the European Union acts as a surrogate state, i.e. has the power to regulate and rationalise… Notionally, this extension of EU power is consensual but in reality it derives from agreements among elites and generates two sets of problems. The extension is simultaneously contested and welcomed. At the core of the EU is the process that once its member states have ceded power to it, the EU applies them autonomously without further reference to the member states. The inference to be drawn is that the EU is currently operating as an identity-forming process. It is seeking to create an order and a coherence of its own; societies respond to this rationalisation and to that extent become more alike: the outcome is European identity (Schöpflin, 2000: 32–3).

This stance is highlighted by a decision made by the German Federal Constitutional Court (*Bundesverfassungsgericht*) in 1996. The Court ruled it to be unconstitutional to transfer constitutional state functions to the European Union. The judges explained that in order to be legitimate, political and constitutional action by the European Union had to be controllable through democratic participation. Such participation was seen as present within the member states but not yet on the transnational level of the EU (cf. Bruha, 1997: 103–4).

I do not intend to pursue the problem of the often lamented lack of democratic control of EU institutions, which would need to be addressed separately. My concern here is a different one. If one accepts the idea that coming to terms with diversity is the pivotal point of European integration, then the questions arise as to how to establish a common basis; a common communicative space for Europeans to negotiate their perspectives on the future shape of the EU – both culturally and politically – and how this space should be structured. To put it in a nutshell: diversity begs the question of democratic legitimacy. Democratic legitimacy, since it is founded on information and opinion, requires communication. This implies and presupposes cultural and political literacy – and the linguistic ability to participate in these discourses.

The Structure of a European Public Space

In an essay on the question whether linguistic plurality will eventually be the limiting factor for European democracy, Beierwaltes (1998: 11, my translation) writes 'that a common language could well strengthen the communicative integration of a community but that such a degree of homogeneity would not be required as an absolute precondition for a European public space and thus for European democracy'. His aim is to sketch a 'topography of a public space'. Set in opposition to a holistic understanding of the term 'public space', according to which each individual – in a prescriptive sense – ought to have the opportunity and ability to enter the discourse (p. 14, my translation), Beierwaltes favours the concept of 'segmented levels of public discourse'. In modernised societies, public space is highly fragmented even on the national level. In order to describe the fault lines of public segmentation, Beierwaltes borrows a model from Gerhards and Neidhardt. They develop a model of public fori on three levels, which differ in structure and their institutional and technological prerequisites (pp. 14–16, my translation):

(1) The level of public encounters, which is very loosely structured and comprises coincidental communication with a wide spectrum of possible topics.
(2) The level of public assemblies, which is topic-related and structurally more determined through participants and speakers. This type of public forum relies on the freedom of assembly, speech and opinion.
(3) The level of the public mass media, which requires an appropriate technological infrastructure including specialists (e.g. journalists). The freedom of the press is an additional prerequisite.

All three levels play a vital role in the public control of political decision-making processes and cannot be substituted for one another or dispensed with altogether. Nonetheless, they are only loosely interconnected. On the transnational, European level, the complexity of the situation is increased through the number of different languages because they reduce internal and intensive interconnection of public fori of similar structure and function (p. 26).

What needs to be done? 'The decisive question therefore is… what the challenges are if we want to see the central function of control assured within a European context' (p. 20; my translation). In order to initiate and continue the integration of European, national and local public spaces, Beierwaltes lists three main measures which need to be considered simultaneously:

(1) Transparency of the political system;
(2) European contextualisation of national public fori;
(3) Strengthening of communicative integration.

It is vital to understand that these are not isolated measures but highly complex processes that require action on many levels. Kettner and Schneider argue in a similar way that

> the construction of co-operative political institutions will remain insufficient without the development of a political public; and that, vice versa, public political communication, which functions as a provider for information and transparency only, cannot fulfil high demands for structures of democratic governance if it is not linked with procedures of substantial control and responsibility (2000: 369, my translation).

It seems to me that a horizontal connection of European public spaces on all three levels (encounter, assembly, mass media) requires competent citizens in two specific ways which I shall discuss in the following section.

Cultural Literacy and Participation

European Integration has become much more than the challenge to harmonise economies and national law. It has also become a process concerning the structure of people's social integration and individual identity. The traditional ways of national and cultural integration have received a new sibling which extends on to the European level. Highly modernised societies, such as the Western European nation states, increasingly require their members to cope with the claims of multiple membership:

> The classic order of the western nation state is centred around formal equality in the sense of uniform citizenship rights. Citizenship assumes a single status; all citizens are entitled to the same rights and privileges. The post-national model, on the other hand, implies multiplicity of membership – a principal organisational form for empires and city states (Soysal, 1996: 22).

As one consequence of multiple membership, multiple loyalties need to be generated by the European citizen (Münch, 1999: 471 ff.; Schlesinger, 1994: 321; Schöpflin, 2000: 30). Here, the abstract task of coping with diversity is echoed in the challenge for the individual to construct his or her identity within a manifold network of different frames. The ties that bind will arguably have to be knit with respect to a new, transnational frame of reference. It seems to me, therefore, to be a key competence to integrate these claims for identity in a non-conflicting manner. In order to do so, the individual will have to be enabled to generate categories of cultural reference beyond the nation.

Meißner defines culture, citing Niklas Luhmann, as 'a common repertoire of representative themes and experiences, which are topical in a given society with some frequency' (1996: 54, my translation). For Meißner, the specifically European dimension of foreign language learning could then be described as to enable students to experience first-hand participation in foreign discourses without the distorting intervention of translation. This type of multilateral participation in communication would ideally lead to an authentic understanding of foreign modes of choice of themes and of opinion formation and can thus be seen, from a pedagogical point of view, as a form of 'tertiary socialisation' (cf. also Byram, 1989; Doyé, 1992).

In my view, this implies an awareness of the determining influence of culture on how the (social) world is perceived and mentally constructed, and of how these influences are dynamic in their ability to continually restructure reality. This is what I should like to call 'cultural literacy'. Maybe this is one answer to the challenge of multiple identification and loyalties.

European Communicative Integration

European communicative integration is part of the more comprehensive process of European Integration. Communicative integration leads back to the question of unity and diversity. In democracies, legitimacy of power is based on opinion – and opinion requires language and knowledge about language (cf. Meißner, 1996: 50). In consequence, Meißner's appeal is for a solid knowledge of a number of languages within their cultural and historical contexts. He believes that translation in general subjects any transnational discourse to cultural distortion, which should be avoided in order to establish a proper understanding. Beierwaltes, similarly, argues that one single common language for a transnational European public space would not necessarily be required, as different levels of such a space exist with different linguistic requirements. It seems reasonable to me to presume that transnational communication will be most likely to occur on two out of the three levels described by Beierwaltes. With increasing mobility, people will meet and develop communicative needs within situations of personal encounters. Increasing economic and political interdependence necessitates mass media communication. Meißner and Beierwaltes, coming from different directions, both argue against a deterministic attitude that only a European lingua franca will eventually guarantee further and complete integration. But maybe it should be emphasised that the absence of common linguistic grounds may result in what can be described as 'isolation in diversity'. In a situation of political deliberation where communicative needs are not bi- or trilateral but plurilateral, diversity can be counterproductive if it results in speechlessness. Avoiding the lingua franca trap is, therefore, only one part of the answer to the problem. Oommen (1997: 203) points at both sides of the coin:

> Finally, the importance of communication for developing a participative polity should be squarely endorsed as a prerequisite. In spite of this, multi-national polities should have several national languages even if they limit the number of official languages to a workable minimum.

Beierwaltes' view that one common language is no *absolute* prerequisite to European integration as a participative polity can be supported – just as Oommen's consideration that functioning communication *is*.

It may have become clear that communicative integration requires finding the delicate balance between linguistic unity and linguistic diversity. The emergence of a European public sphere will require both. Neither will suffice, and neither can be dispensed with. Linguistic diversity as an educational goal can certainly help to make the European Union more easily acceptable for the people of Europe. As a polity, the EU will of necessity gradually adopt constitutional functions presently reserved for the sovereignty of the individual member states. Therefore, it will be necessary to subject this process to democratic deliberation, in which linguistic and national identities are respected in the sense that they continue to be a part of people's identities. In a practical sense, this means that their languages must be functional within a European discursive sphere.

The looming fragmentation of such a European discursive sphere might be met in a twofold way. Firstly, multilingual education would need to become a set goal of state controlled education. Secondly, the dominance of English should not be deplored. It would indeed be difficult to understand why in most European countries English is taught on an obligatory basis and why at the same time it should not be acknowledged as a language which can be *used for a purpose*. Instead, English might be seen as a viable linguistic option which allows competent partners to negotiate their positions within a discourse. As a consequence,

Janssen (1999) argues that English language proficiency is indispensable since any form of 'broken or fragmented "Euro-English"' would give rise to language conflict:

> Thus, if the teaching of English is restricted to selected parts of the communicative competence in English and of the English language system, this can be expected to strengthen a covert *linguicism* in Europe. Furthermore, neither of these solutions ['an English-based system of "minimal communication", a restriction of English to only receptive abilities' (Janssen: 41) SB] sufficiently reflects the influence of social and cultural attitudes on learning a foreign (not simply, a second) language – in particular, the New Localism accompanied by the negative tendency of increasing linguistic and cultural distance. Neglecting these attitudes could provoke severe language conflicts and the establishment of new and more negative attitudes towards the English language and/or the implementation of English from outside or above, which in turn could then only be experienced as a kind of *linguistic imperialism*. It should once again be emphasised that it is not the English language that will cause conflicts but the conversational and attitudinal *use* of it, particularly when applied without negotiation within a discourse, and, above all, the decisive step to restrict the teaching to deficient competences (p. 51).

If linguistic diversity can usefully be seen to counterbalance the gravitational force which emanates from English as a lingua franca, English may function as a direct mediator between participants in a discourse who would otherwise have to rely on translation. Furthermore, English already is the very linguistic means to give speakers, especially of lesser-used languages, their voice within a European public discourse. In summary, linguistic diversity and the use of English as a form of lingua franca very probably rely on each other. They are not at all mutually exclusive. Rather the opposite seems to be the case. As Janssen points out, if the teaching of English as the most common 'default' foreign language also implies teaching what he calls 'extended communicative competence' (p. 52), it may even become more likely for other languages to enter the discourse:

> Teaching English this way... is by no means linked to *linguicism*, but could support an unrestricted way of language choice on the levels of micro- and macro-situations. Speakers are enabled to maintain their native (local) language and cultural identity, but at the same time become capable of using different languages without fear they might lose their own identity and language (Janssen, 1999: 53).

If the political and educational aim is geared towards communicative integration in Europe, both factors, linguistic unity and linguistic diversity, have to be taken into account. European communicative integration is in itself a function of the process of European integration in a more general sense. Communicative integration again centres on the development of a European public sphere where a discourse of deliberation of future political and cultural perspectives can evolve. Its various levels, national and transnational, become accessible through English on the one hand and through competence in other languages on the other. To my mind, the acceptance of integration by European citizens depends to a large extent on their ability and willingness to participate in a European public discourse. Here, proficiency in English as a possible and reliable interlingual mediator and the equality of people's linguistic identities are interdependent factors which both originate in the history of modern Europe and thus require their place in the present discussion. Throughout its history, Europe has seen more than one disastrously failed attempt to homogenise its peoples and cultures. It would indeed be odd to find the problem of communicative integration a straightforward and non-paradoxical one.

Correspondence

Any correspondence should be directed to Stephan Briedbach, Universität Bremen, Fachbereich 10, Postfach 330440, 28344 Bremen, Germany (sbreidbach@uni-bremen.de).

References

Albisetti, J. (1993) The debate on secondary school reform in France and Germany. In D.K. Müller, F. Ringer and B. Simon (eds) *The Rise of the Modern Educational System. Structural Change and Social Reproduction 1870–1920* (pp. 181–96). Cambridge: Cambridge University Press; Paris: Editions de la Maison des Sciences de l'Homme.
Arntz, R. (1998) *Das Vielsprachige Europa. Eine Herausforderung für Sprachpolitik und Sprachplanung*. Hildesheim: Universitätsbibliothek Hildesheim.
Barbour, S. and Carmichael, C. (eds) (2000) *Language and Nationalism in Europe*. Oxford: Oxford University Press.
Beierwaltes, A. (1998) *Sprachenvielfalt in der EU – Grenze einer Demokratisierung Europas?* Bonn: Centre for European Integration Studies.
Bifulco, M. (1998) *In Search of an Identity for Europe*. Bonn: Centre for European Integration Studies.
Bruha, T. (1997) Rechtliche Aspekte der Vielsprachigkeit: Vertrags-, Amts-, Arbeits- und Verkehrssprachen in der Europäischen Union. In T. Bruha and H.-J. Seeler (eds) *Die Europäische Union und ihre Sprachen*. Interdisziplinäres Symposium zu Vielsprachigkeit als Herausforderung und Problematik des europäischen Einigungsprozesses. Gespräch zwischen Wissenschaft und Praxis (pp. 83–104). Baden Baden: Nomos.
Byram, M. (1989) Intercultural education and foreign language teaching. *World Studies Journal* 7 (2), 4–7.
Christ, H. (1993) *Fremdsprachenpolitik für das Jahr 2000. Sprachenpolitische Betrachtungen zum Lehren und Lernen fremder Sprachen*. Tübingen: Narr.
Christ, I. (1998) Lernziel Mehrsprachigkeit. In J. Pleines (ed.) *Sprachen und mehr. Globale Kommunikation als Herausforderung* (pp. 210–17). Wiesbaden: Harrassowitz.
Council of Europe (1998) Recommendation 98(6) of the Committee of Ministers on *Linguistic Diversity*.
Doyé, P. (1992) Fremdsprachenunterricht als Beitrag zu tertiärer Sozialisation. In D. Buttjes, W. Butzkamm and F. Klippel (eds) *Neue Brennpunkte des Englischunterrichts* (pp. 280–95). Frankfurt/M.: Lang.
Eurobarometer. Europeans and Languages. Eurobarometer Report 54. 15th February 2001. http://europa.eu.int/comm/education/languages.html
European Commission (1995) White Paper on Education and Training – Teaching and Learning – Towards the Learning Society. COM(95)590. http://europa.eu.int/en/record/white/edu9511/
Eurostat. News Release No 53/2001, 17 May 2001. http://europa.eu.int/comm/eurostat.html
Gogolin, I. (1994) *Der Monolinguale Habitus der Multilingualen Schule*. Münster; New York: Waxmann.
Hutchinson, J. (1994) Cultural nationalism and moral regeneration. In J. Hutchinson and A.D. Smith (eds) *Nationalism* (pp. 122–31). Oxford: Oxford University Press.

Hutchinson, J. (1987) *The Dynamics of Cultural Nationalism*. London: Allen and Unwin.

Hutchinson, J. and Smith, A.D. (eds.) (1994) *Nationalism*. Oxford: Oxford University Press.

Janssen, H. (1999) Linguistic dominance or acculturation – problems of teaching English as a global language. In C. Gnutzmann (ed.) *Teaching and Learning English as a Global Language: Native and Non-Native Perspectives* (pp. 41–55). Tübingen: Stauffenburg.

Jeske, C.M. (2000) Europäische Mehrsprachigkeit – Möglichkeiten und Grenzen. *Fremdsprachen Lehren und Lernen* 29, 179–90.

Kettner, M. and Schneider, M.-L. (2000) Öffentlichkeit und entgrenzter politischer Handlungsraum: Der Traum von der 'Weltöffentlichkeit' und die Lehren des europäischen Publizitätsproblems. In H. Brunkhorst and M. Kettner (eds) *Globalisierung und Demokratie. Wirtschaft, Recht, Medien* (pp. 369–411). Frankfurt/M.: Suhrkamp.

Meißner, F.-J. (1996) Multikulturalität, Multilateralität, Eurokulturalität – Orientierungen für einen europäischen Fremdsprachenunterricht. In H. Christ and M. Legutke (eds) *Fremde Texte verstehen*. Festschrift für Lothar Bredella (pp. 50–61). Tübingen: Narr.

Meißner, F.-J. (1998) Umrisse einer Mehrsprachigkeitsdidaktik. In L. Bredella (ed.) *Verstehen und Verständigung durch Sprachenlernen* (pp. 172–87). Bochum: Brockmeyer.

Münch, R. (1999) Europäische Identitätsbildung. Zwischen globaler Dynamik, nationaler und regionaler Gegenbewegung. In H. Willems and A. Hahn (eds) *Identität und Moderne* (pp. 465–86). Frankfurt/M.: Suhrkamp.

Oommen, T.K. (1997) *Citizenship, Nationality and Ethnicity. Reconciling Competing Identities*. Cambridge: Polity Press.

Paulston, C.B. (1994) *Linguistic Minorities in Multilingual Settings*. Amsterdam; Philadelphia: Benjamins.

Raasch, A. (1999) Breaking down borders – through languages. In H.-J. Krumm (ed.) *The Languages of our Neighbours – Our Languages*. Proceedings of the Symposium, Vienna 29. 10. – 31. 10. 1998 (pp. 78–91). Vienna: Eviva.

Schlesinger, P. (1994) Europeanness: A new cultural battlefield? In J. Hutchinson and A.D. Smith (eds) *Nationalism* (pp. 316–25). Oxford: Oxford University Press.

Schöpflin, G. (2000) *Nations, Identity, Power: The New Politics of Europe*. London: Hurst and Company.

Seeler, H.-J. (1997) Begrüßung und Einführung. In T. Bruha and H.-J. Seeler (eds) *Die Europäische Union und ihre Sprachen*. Interdisziplinäres Symposium zu Vielsprachigkeit als Herausforderung und Problematik des europäischen Einigungsprozesses. Gespräch zwischen Wissenschaft und Praxis (pp. 9–13). Baden Baden: Nomos.

Soysal, Y.N. (1996) Changing citizenship in Europe. Remarks on postnational membership and the national state. In D. Cesarani and M. Fulbrook (eds) *Citizenship, Nationality and Migration in Europe* (pp. 17–29). London; New York: Routledge.

Vollmer, H.J. (2001) Englisch und Mehrsprachigkeit: Interkulturelles Lernen durch Englisch als lingua franca? In D. Abendroth-Timmer and G. Bach (eds) *Mehrsprachiges Europa*. Festschrift für Michael Wendt zum 60. Geburtstag (pp. 91–109). Tübingen: Narr.

Context, Culture and Construction: Research Implications of Theory Formation in Foreign Language Methodology[1]

Michael Wendt

Universität Bremen, Fachbereich 10, Postfach 330440, 28334 Bremen, Germany

Language is learnt in context and any approach to research on language learning needs to take this fully into account. A constructivist theory of context includes both internal and external realities, and research methods are needed which can investigate the ways in which mental processes turn reality into contexts. Traditional research paradigms that rely on concepts of objectivity are unable to deal with this theory of context and qualitative research methods also need to be reappraised for their viability in investigating language learning. The purpose of this article is to consider to what extent constructivist epistemology provides a solution for achieving a link between qualitative-ethnographic and cognitivist research on foreign language acquisition. The conclusion points to the validity of qualitative research provided that there is clarity and explicitness of process so that those who read research can carry out their own interpretations.

The European Research Programme 'Processes of Language Acquisition in Multiple Environments', in which universities of five different countries are involved, is based on the desideratum of integrating research on mental processes and research on contexts of language acquisition. This article starts from the assumption that during the last decade institutional learning contexts have become more flexible and that in the same period the focus has shifted from the teaching ritual to the learner and his/her mental processes. Presuming that insightful learning is closely connected to understanding, the author introduces central aspects of epistemological constructivism, which explains perception as the construction of meaning in educational and cultural contexts. In the fourth part we demonstrate that a number of traditional quantitative and qualitative research methods are not suitable for examining mental processes, contexts and their interdependence. Finally, we recommend the consideration of constructivist principles in research. This way of proceeding requires a disturbing change of ideas, which is worthwhile, however, for it helps us to understand language learning and acquisition better.

Language Learning Processes and Their Contexts

Prior to the triumphal march of the language laboratory in the sixties of the last century, instructional contexts of language learning were basically confined to teacher-centred teaching, language-embedding textbooks and traditional ways of visualisation. They were supplemented by more or less canonical, authorised reading matter, which was to provide access to authentic accounts of the target culture. In the last decades, previously familiar teaching and learning contexts were reorganised to be more flexible, more complex and – in a certain sense – more authentic through other forms of social interaction, of which – in a broader sense – tandem learning is also a part (cf. Bechtl, 2001). The new organisation of contexts was also achieved through the development of diverse learning environments, through learning software and the internet. Above all, the opportunities for information and communication provided by the internet can contribute to a globalisation of learning contexts (Müller-Hartmann, 2001: 207ff.).

There was, in the same period, a noteworthy development which addressed the requirement for learner orientation and facilitated learning through action. Initial practical consequences ensued from the further development of the concept of a closed situation in the audio-visual phase to the open concept in communicative methods. Whereas cultural studies, role play, simulation, debates about authenticity and early forms of intercultural learning were exclusively oriented towards the target context, the individual learners, their contexts of origin and their individual learning processes were already at the heart of discussion in communicative methods (cf. Schüle, 1995: 78, 84), in holistic learning concepts, later in specific forms of encouraging creativity (e.g. Mummert, 1991), in productive forms of dealing with texts (*rewriting*) as well as in strategies for the development of learner autonomy and independent study (e.g. Lahaie, 1995). Today they are a central part in the autonomy debate and in constructivist methodology (Wendt, 1993, 1996, 2000a). It was left to only very few experts in teaching methods (Byram, 1994; Doyé, 1992) to particularly emphasise that the – at least – temporary participation in everyday life of the target culture is indispensable for intercultural learning as a process of socialisation.

Research on foreign language learning should take into account both of these fundamental directions in foreign language teaching methods. It should examine how and with regard to which theoretical principles the research on the learning *context* and the learning *process* can be combined. In the following section we attempt to show in which way this could be successful.

Epistemological Constructivism

Living in two worlds: External and mental realities

The modelling of a holistic view of context and mental processes is the crucial element of the approaches which have emerged from epistemological constructivism. It can only be presented in outline here (see Wendt, 1993, 1996, 2000b for further discussion).

Contrary to popular belief, epistemological ('radical') constructivism does not call into question reality as such. In a quotation from Schütz and Luckmann (1979: 25f.), Hu (2001: 29) emphasises one sentence in bold print, which could be accepted by epistemological constructivists as well: 'Die Welt ist für den Menschen in der natürlichen Einstellung niemals eine bloße Ansammlung von Farbflecken, unzusammenhängenden Geräuschen oder Zentren von kalt und warm'. (For the human being in his/her natural attitude, the world is never a mere accumulation of coloured spots, isolated noises or centres of cold and heat.) This makes it perfectly clear that the well-regulated nature of perceptible reality can only be established by appeal to a corresponding attitude – an attitude that must be assigned to an interpreting, thus mental view of the world. In a similar manner, Karl Popper (1972/1994: 75) has in his three-world-model already distinguished between a physical world (World 1) and the world of our interpretations, which has to be regarded as a subjective world of consciousness (World 3 is disregarded here as it contains trivial truths in the realm of logic with no equivalents in World 1).

Entirely in accord with this, epistemological constructivism starts from the assumption of an ontological difference of reality on the one hand and knowledge about reality on the other hand. The necessity to distinguish both has played an important role in the history of philosophy, among others in Vico's work, in the British empiricists (cf. Glasersfeld, 1992b) and in Kant's, Heidegger's and Sartre's differentiations of the forms of being 'an sich' and 'für sich'.

In other words, if we claim from a 'realistic' standpoint that we know something about reality, we change from World 1 to World 2, which is a mental world whose states interact with each other (the self-referential character of the cognitive system) and which we thereafter designate as 'reality'. Inasmuch that it is image-like, we can speak of 'imagination' in the original meaning of the word.

Constructivists consider this 'reality' to be a subjective mental construction guiding our actions in the external reality. Should it not fulfil this task and hence not be viable (meaning here: functional), we have to change or enlarge it. Ensuring the viability of subjective constructions in communication is the basis of inter-subjective or 'social' constructions of 'reality'.

Hence, reality is the area in which our mental processes occur. A particularly important process is the construction of meaning, as is shown in the following section.

Perception is interpretation

Undoubtedly, our sense organs are capable of receiving energetic impulses from reality. But the structure of the field of perception in Gestalt-theory terms, differentiation and recognition of similarities, are cognitive abilities which have to be developed in the course of ontogenesis. Semir Zeki (1999), a neuro-biologist from London, has shown in detail that seeing is basically a form of thinking.

From a constructivist point of view, meaning is not a perceptible feature of reality, nor of a succession of sounds or written characters. But in order to survive, we are used to assigning meaning to, to interpreting, all objects and circumstances, from childhood onwards. Therefore, meaning is a quality of the mental world and is likewise permanently checked for viability through individuation and socialisation. Subjective meanings are called 'connotative' and those which have been made viable through communication 'denotative'.

The concept of meaning presented here is a holistic one, since it is connected to cognitive, affective and physical experiences. It is justified by the assumption that we interpret everything we not only recognise, but consciously perceive. Hu's formulation is in accord with this view (2001: 24): 'Die Welt der Menschen ist eine Welt der Bedeutungen, eine immer schon interpretierte Welt.' (The world of human beings is a world of meanings which is always already interpreted.)

Context as 'Cause'

If we, as was just explained, always perceive reality as interpreted reality, the objectivity of perception appears to be questionable. This problem has been commented on in different ways from different perspectives.

The discussion of research methodology in foreign language teaching and in research on foreign language learning is still strongly influenced by the information processing paradigm in its different forms (cf. McLaughlin & Heredia, 1996; Grotjahn, 1997: 35–8, 1999; cf. Segermann, 1996; Wendt, 2000b: 17–21). In its conception of the world, reality provides objective information incorporated by the brain as input (Pishwa, 1998: 13) or intake and processed with reference to existing experiences, similar to the processes inside a computer. Even though it remains unclear what 'information' is (Grotjahn, 1997: 35), objective knowledge is regarded as possible.

Hermeneutics and reception pragmatics (cf. Köpf, 1981) believe in objective knowledge only to a limited extent. Since Dilthey, the scientific observer is seen as bound to their historical context ('situation') influencing their view of the subject.

According to Popper, context belongs to World 1; this world transmits signals and 'insists' on being interpreted by us. According to the position outlined above, however, signals are not objective facts since they have to be perceived and interpreted in the process of perception. Consequently, all that can be claimed is that contexts are 'causes' for interpretations and that perceived contexts are always interpreted contexts (products of interpretation). From this it follows that concrete, social and communicative contexts have to be regarded as 'causes' for the construction of meaningful realities and for checking their viability. 'Understanding' has then to be described as the mental constructing of hypothetical, sense-making relations between signals from an already interpreted reality.

Hence, semantic domains of reference are not real, but already interpreted and therefore mental contexts. Foreign language instruction has to deal with these contexts when wanting to provide learning contexts and to promote context sensitivity. And if the description of the learners' realities in their cognitive, emotional and physical state (Hu, 2001: 22) is regarded as a task of language acquisition research, it has to direct its attention towards the external reality of the learners as interpreted context and towards their mental reality as interpreting context.

Culture as a Discursive Construct

Contexts and their interpretations are usually understood as being culturally determined. Therefore, the question arises how 'culture' has to be defined from a constructivist perspective. As it is impossible to discuss the great number of existing definitions individually, we start from the basic convictions they are founded on.

There are two fundamentally different conceptions of culture at the heart of the debate in philosophy, sociology and cultural studies, which is currently being joined by foreign language methodology. On the one hand, culture is seen as a distinguishable, homogeneous and objectively describable or 'essentialist' system. On the other hand, it is understood as dynamically developing events which are consequently only seized as momentary perceptions.

The first point of view has dominated the discussion of intercultural learning for a long time and is still the basis of many approaches to teaching and the metaphors related to them; for example this is true of Finkbeiner and Koplin's software and iceberg metaphors. Only the argument between Edmondson and House (1998) and Hu (1999) has made more open conceptions, compatible with post-modern theories, worth considering as more process-oriented alternatives for foreign language teaching methodology. Since, in an immigration and information society, each individual participates in several cultures, these and the categories 'own' and 'foreign' cannot be seen as objective facts, according to Hu (1999, 2001: 23). It has to be assumed that cultures constitute themselves dynamically in discourse.

A discourse-analytical notion of culture would support the distinction between macro contexts (organisations, institutions) and micro contexts made by Wodak (1996). It would also facilitate the notion of the classroom 'as a culture constituted through the interaction of teachers and learners' (Müller-Hartmann, 2001: 215).

Furthermore, it should be taken into consideration that – according to Fairclough's *Critical Discourse Analysis* – discourses are always structured hegemonically. And here we encounter the question in how far communicative power can be exercised. From the point of view of epistemological constructivism, this presupposes the acceptance of the hegemonic interpretation of the discourse context by the potential victim, and the latter's willingness to move towards the constructions of reality of more powerful constructors. The exertion of communicative power on people living in different constructions of reality and not willing to question them (e.g. neo-Nazis, martyrs, terrorists, kamikaze-warriors or guerrilla fighters) must be regarded as almost impossible.

The consequences for the forms of inquiry currently customary in qualitative research should also be considered.

Hu (2001: 23f.) accepts Geertz' (1991: 9) semiotic-interpretive notion of culture: 'Believing, with Max Weber, that man is an animal suspended in webs of significance which he himself has spun, I take culture to be those webs'. On this basis one could, in Hu's view (2001: 24), still examine collective structures of meaning, or place differences within individual points of view at the centre of attention; in the latter case, conversations with individual persons would allow conclusions to be drawn as to personal patterns of interpretation.

Geertz does not only acknowledge individual 'webs of significance', but also social ones. Therefore he (1987: 46) describes culture as a historically handed down system of meanings occurring in symbolic form. On this basis it would be possible to communicate, maintain and develop knowledge and attitudes. Communication is here clearly understood in terms of information processing theory.

From a constructivist point of view, primary ontogenetic and individual meanings are only integrated in socially shared meanings insofar as it is necessary to ensure their viability in processes of interaction. Thus there is always a clearly visible 'remainder' of individual connotative meaning indispensable for one's own world view and understanding of self. It is still sensible to distinguish between the individual and their meanings on the one hand and culture as the semantic dimension of a group on the other hand – even if individually interpreted social patterns of perception are often used for checking the viability of individual patterns of perception.

Consequently, culture has to be defined as the denotative level of meaning of social and communicative interaction. Processes of socialisation, acculturation and integration – understood here as the opposite of exclusion in the Freudian concept of culture (cf. Hartmann, 2000) – as well as processes of individualisation in the sense of socio-cultural self-perception are founded on ensuring the viability of connotative meanings in social contexts.

The formation of Maturana's (1978: passim) 'consensual areas' can be used as a metaphor for the totality of these events. It figuratively characterises the human being's journey from their original alienation into society. Being foreign or different, however, always remains, to a certain degree, irrevocable in post-structuralist and deconstructivist theories as well as in Hunfeld (1998).

This is not to advocate a dichotomy of 'own' and 'foreign' corresponding to an essentialist viewpoint of traditional concepts of intercultural learning which tend to be ideological. 'Own' and 'foreign' are not objective categories, but individual and inter-individual patterns of perception which are made viable, i.e. they seem to function. A high potential for (self-) identification and a high discourse value can be attributed to those patterns.

In these circumstances, intercultural learning is seen as a transgression of limits of socialisation into primary communities and a move towards 'the foreign', which is accepted as a potential 'authority' for ensuring viability (Wendt, 1993). Foreign language instruction can contribute to this by conveying the understanding that one's own as well as the foreign culture are constructs ('construction awareness').

The new understanding of 'context' includes the mental processes which turn reality into contexts. Since these cannot be regarded as objective, the question as to whether traditional research paradigms can cope with this extended notion is explored in the following section.

Research Theory and Practice

The qualitative paradigm and the varieties of reality

First of all, let us emphasise that qualitative and quantitative methods correspond to different views of the world and different epistemological interests.

Quantitative procedures reduce context, mental realities and cognitive processes to quantifiable data often presented as input/intake or output against the background of the information processing model. The reduction to representative indicators and controllable variables is done to ensure the generalisability of the results, which are interpreted as covering laws on the basis of assumptions about causality.

Whereas in this paradigm abstractions are made from the individual case in order to compare as many cases as possible, what matters in qualitative research is the holistic description of concrete people and specific contexts (cf. Lamnek, 1988: 242ff. for an overview). Although this leads to the abandoning of typification and to acceptance of the uniqueness of the individual, and therefore to the exclusion of any generalisability or even transfer, nonetheless it has the advantage of contributing to the description of *one* possibility or variety of 'reality'.

Whereas quantitative research requires the testing of hypotheses, which once formulated must not be changed throughout data collection and analysis in order to make it possible to refute them, the, in a positive sense, exploratory description of uniqueness requires a research process in which there is a constant succession of hypothesis construction and testing during data collection, especially in data analysis. Research methods corresponding to this process, called *progressive focusing* (Grau, 2001: 69ff.) go back to *grounded theory* (cf. Strauss & Corbin, 1990; Titscher *et al.*, 1998: 94).

Müller-Hartmann and Schocker-von Ditfurth (2001b: 6) consider the exploration of collective and diverging sense structures to be a task for qualitative research, but there are certain limitations. Qualitative cultural research – above all – has to focus on individual processes of meaning construction for which interpreted collective structures of meaning and contexts form reassuring authorities.

Since in recent years there has been in cognitive theory oriented foreign language methodology an accumulation of neurobiological findings (cf. Bleyhl, 1998), we must emphasise at this point the problematic nature of interpretation in this kind of research. Not only does this problem result from the nomothetic and – as a rule – quantitative orientation of this research, but also from the unverified assumption of a physiological basis for highly complex cognitive processes ('physicalism': Hutto, 2000).

In conclusion, research attempting to document contexts as interpreted realities cannot refrain from qualitative methods. Yet who are the interpreting subjects?

Subjectivity and authenticity

The reality of contexts is an external reality interpreted by an observer. This holds true for all participants in the research process. It demands from the researcher the depiction of his/her own reality, which in turn has to be regarded as an interpretation as well, and which according to Foerster (1996: 15) is a requirement which is being accepted increasingly in all forms of scientific research. From this standpoint, qualitative research appears to be the most extensive analysis of the interpretations of the subjects who are interacting in the research process.

In her article on 'subjectivity and exploration of authentic perspectives', Hu (2001: 11) is concerned with the delimitation of cognitivist and ethnographic approaches. Since she does not regard language acquisition as an individual process and considers learning as above all social action in socio-cultural contexts (pp. 15, 17, 22), her ethnographic research approaches seem to be more promising than the subject-oriented exploration of mental processes. In my opinion, however, a position not taking into consideration both the socio-cultural as well as the individual-mental dimension of language acquisition comes close to behaviourism rehabilitated on the basis of social contexts.

Hu (p. 24) certainly accepts the subjectivity of the persons interacting in the research process. Nonetheless, she (p. 28) postulates the ability of these persons to present their reality authentically. She justifies this point of view in terms of the ethics of research with the right of the 'researched' individuals to be taken seriously (p. 29), and in theoretical terms with reference to phenomenologically oriented positions (p. 29). These presume an objective world next to the subjectively perceived world, but neglect the processes initiated by and again influencing the perception of this world.

This attempt to 'save' authenticity for an ethnographic research approach does not seem appropriate for combining research on context and research on cognition. With regard to research theory as well as foreign language methodology, it is much more advisable to see authenticity as a quality mark attributed to facts which seem to constitute a genuine element of a field of perception or cognition. Hence, these facts can be regarded as preferential for scrutinising the viability of our constructions of reality.

Ethnomethodology and ethnography

If as suggested above, we regard culture as the denotative context of subjective-connotative constructions of meaning and of the check on their viability, some basic assumptions of ethnomethodology and ethnography appear in a different light.

Ethnomethodology – above all based on the works of Garfinkel (1967, 1972, etc.) – attempts to reconstruct the explanatory and interpretive patterns of the members of a community and with this their patterns of perception. Meaning, social realities and social orders are produced 'locally' and ratified inter-subjectively (cf. Titscher *et al.*, 1998: 121ff.). 'Locally' refers to the status of contexts. Nevertheless, these are not objectively given; they are part of the process of interaction: actions and contexts are mutually constituted . This 'reflexive context orientation' is to a large degree compatible with the social construction of reality in constructivist approaches (e.g. Hejl, 1992).

A very careful evaluation, however, requires a text analysis procedure which is the preference in ethnomethodology. Pragmatic discourse analysis often conceals an essentialist view of everyday culture. Furthermore, Titscher *et al.* (1998) question whether such analyses can be successful without any prerequisites, especially since the analytic categories are defined by the researcher.

Qualitative ethnographic research in the tradition of Gumperz and Hymes (1964) analyses speech, text and non-verbal expressions against the background of cultural structures or it attempts to reveal cultural structures with the help of texts. Analyses of individual cases or small groups (e.g. *Systematic Multiple Level Observation of Groups* according to Bales & Cohen, 1982) are the order of the day. Situational, non-verbal and biographical contexts are regarded as constitutive for speech acts (Hymes, 1979: 47ff.; Fitch & Philipsen, 1995; so-called 'cultural pragmatics').

Problems primarily arise from two principles of data collection founded on an understanding of reality on which there is insufficient reflection. 'Thick description' (cf. Auer, 1999) has to record complexity, multiple voices (Hu, 2001: 33) and contradictions, and its purpose is to ensure generalisability as well as external and internal validity (Schlak, 2000: 15ff., 20f.). According to constructivist views, mental reality also constitutes an essential element of each research object. However, language does not refer to real contexts, but to their interpretation through the subject. A conception which regards reality as independent of the researcher's assumptions is incompatible with this understanding (cf. among others Titscher *et al.*, 1998: 115).

'Participant observation' promotes, hence the 'verstehende Beschreibung der

Innensicht der zu dieser Kultur gehörenden Personen, deren Lebenswelt der Forscherin möglichst vertraut werden soll' (the 'understanding description of the inside perspective of people belonging to the culture studied, with which the researcher should become as familiar as possible'; Schocker-von Ditfurth, 2001: 96). Thus, it demands the adoption of a social role in the research field. Researchers have to retire so far into the background that they become learners (Schlak, 2000: 69). Whereas in ethnographic approaches the researcher very widely accommodates to his/her research subject and its context (Titscher *et al.*, 1998: 115), from a constructivist point of view, the observer perspective constitutes an essential dimension of the cognitive and the research process.

Both ethnomethodological as well as qualitative-ethnographic research are founded on a theoretical concept of information processing which does not differentiate between contexts and mental processes, and even ignores the latter.

If we consider learning as a process which is 'caused' by context and community, but which nonetheless has to be achieved by the individual themselves, the approaches discussed here require an additional cognitive dimension. To our knowledge, this is – if at all – only possible with the joint interpretation of qualitative data obtainable with introspective methods in the broadest sense – for example, commenting on one's own pictures or techniques of graphic representation – or with interview techniques.

In this context, constructivist semantics provide a model of reality and an appropriate approach to qualitative research on learning, motivation, attitude and intercultural learning. Uttered interpretations as well as reasons given for these are ascertained and connected to individual experiences whenever possible. This holistic view does not tie knowledge, learning, experiences and attitudes to the categories 'cognitive' and/or 'affective', but to their process-oriented nature.

Aspects of a Constructivist Research Theory

Let us summarise here the argument so far. The purpose is to consider to what extent constructivist epistemology provides a solution for achieving a link between qualitative-ethnographic and cognitivist research on foreign language acquisition – as opposed to Hu's (2001) reservations sketched above.

Despite the doubts of some scholars (e.g.Grotjahn, 1999) concerning radical constructivism, epistemological constructivism has at its disposal a research theory with an empirical concept at its centre (cf. among others Krüssel, 1993; Stangl, 1987). Maturana (1978) has outlined from a constructivist point of view the interplay of observation, stating and testing hypotheses. Von Glasersfeld (1992a: 417–31) refers to Hume, Locke and Berkeley according to whom researchers can only test their theories with regard to their experience of the world, but not to the world as such. Similar to Popper (1972), Glaserfeld (1999a: 426f.) deduces from this that a hypothesis only allows an assumption of the possible nature of reality, that a falsified hypothesis, however, can reveal how reality certainly is not. Hence constructivism is not some kind of relativism, but functionalism (Glasersfeld, 1992a: 409).

What is called 'interpretational pattern' by Hu (2001: 24) is seen here as the individual and inter-individual construction of meaning. Not only the social and communicated (Hu, 2001: 31), but also the individually perceived world is an interpreted one. Thus, constructivist research theory has to proceed from the assumption that reality is not input, but rather a 'cause' for constructing meaning and checking its viability (for more detail see Wendt, 2002). As a consequence, only the research participants' interpretations of contexts, the observers' interpretations of contexts, their strategies of construction as well as checking viability are 'real' in an empirical sense. Quantitative research seeing itself as 'objective' can, therefore, only provide causes or opportunities for qualitative research to check on their viability.

As a theory of cognition, epistemological constructivism confronts research on foreign language acquisition with the problem of identifying complex mental processes depending on contextual causes, and of examining to what extent they can be called constructive. Learning and resistance to instruction (Corder, 1981: 8ff.) – seen within the information processing paradigm as sequential acquisition, as intake (Selinker, 1992), or modelled in terms of developmental psychology (Piaget, 1972) – could receive more viable interpretations from a perspective based on the constructive nature of the cognitive system and its self-referential character. Apart from introspective methods, which are indispensable in this regard, learning and reading diaries are among the favoured research methods, as writing can provide motivating occasions for dealing with the learning or reading matter individually and constructively.

As a theory of semantics, epistemological constructivism directs the attention of research related to foreign language learning to the mental constructions of reality. Topics for research corresponding to this perspective include concept formation, attitudes, values, self-assessment, professional concepts, experiential knowledge, subjective theories, concepts of language learning, etc. Context data are provided by biography research, although Finkbeiner and Koplin (2001: 122) refer to autobiographies, diaries and narrative interviews as primary data and biographies and accounts of interviews as secondary data. Mental constructions as such are to some extent explicated in semi-structured interviews.

In line with *grounded theory*, according to which meanings originate from subjective attributions in interaction and are permanently developed and modified (Titscher *et al.*, 1998: 93), and with Hammersley's (1992: 50f.) *respondent validation*, the observer's interpretation of the collected data has to be subjected, in a further step, to the joint checking of its viability by all participants interacting in the research process. The person observed must be given the opportunity to extensively comment on their 'experience' of the research situation. Only in this way can primary inter-subjectivity be achieved to some degree.

Secondary inter-subjectivity is encouraged by the employment of criteria of quality. These are interpretive aids used by the *scientific community* to examine whether research is viable with regard to the paradigms constructed by itself.

In accordance with the above reflections, Riemer (1997: 81) replaces objectivity with inter-subjectivity in her discussion of classic criteria of quality. According to Hu (2001: 30), with embedding into a local, specific context, transferability is no longer a given. The agreement of representation with reality is no longer the central point and multiple truths are assumed (p. 31). Applied to constructivist points of view, this notion of truth refers to the inner consistency of the reality constructions of the individuals interacting in the research process (cf. Rusch, 2001: 74).

Additional quality criteria – e.g. credibility and appropriateness in Schocker-von Ditfurth (2001: 107f.) as well as reliability, operative economy and compatibility in Rusch (2000: 74) – in qualitative and constructivist research theory mainly concern procedures. Thorough documentation of the collected data, 'descriptiveness' (Rusch, 2000), the transparency of the research processes as also required in ethnomethodology (cf. Titscher, 1998: 132), and a multi-perspective view or triangulation respectively (Hammersley, 1992: 50f.) seem to receive most attention.

To sum up from a constructivist point of view, the validity of qualitative research can be presumed if the research process is well-documented so that:

- all steps are comprehensible;
- the mental constructions of all individuals engaged in the research process become clear in the interplay of stating hypotheses and scrutinising their viability in the research process;
- and the reader can carry out their own interpretations.

Is Constructivism 'particularly inconvenient'?

According to Hu (2001: 32), epistemological constructivism calls into question empirical research in a practical discipline and 'sind diese Fragen besonders unbequem' ('these questions are particularly inconvenient').

Traditional research assuming objective facts may indeed be more convenient to handle. Nevertheless, it has not even been able to do justice to a foreign language methodology which is heavily loaded with presentation and input. And this is due to the impossibility of fully accounting for external factors (Stangl, 1987: 336) and of proving linear cause and effect-relations in the field of foreign language learning. It becomes even more implausible with the reinterpretation of learning contexts sketched above as 'causes' for widely self-determined acting and learning.

Therefore, contemporary research has to be prepared to answer exactly these questions about perception of world and self. In search of the processes constituting these perceptions and leading to a specific way of dealing with them, research must not recoil from continuously encountering the learning subject in his/her uniqueness.

Note
1. This article was translated into English by Michael Byram and Britta Viebrock.

Correspondence
Any correspondence should be directed to Dr Michael Wendt, Universität Bremen, Fachbereich 10, Postfach 330440, 28334 Bremen, Germany (inform@uni-bremen.de).

References
Auer, P. (1999) *Sprachliche Interaktion*. Tübingen: Niemeyer.
Bales, R.F. and Cohen, S.P. (1982) *SYMLOG. Ein System für mehrstufige Beobachtung von Gruppen*. Stuttgart: Klett-Cotta.

Bechtel, M. (2001) Zur Erforschung von Aspekten interkulturellen Lernens beim Sprachenlernen im Tandem – Ein diskursanalytischer Ansatz. In A. Müller-Hartmann and M. Schocker-von Ditfurth (eds) *Qualitative Forschung im Bereich Fremdsprachen lehren und lernen* (pp. 264–295). Tübingen: Narr.

Bleyhl, W. (1998) Kognition oder das Selbst-Steuerungs-System auch des Sprachenlerners. In K.-R. Bausch, H. Christ, F.G. Königs and H.J. Krumm (eds) *Kognition als Schlüsselbegriff bei der Erforschung des Lehrens und Lernens fremder Sprachen* (pp. 15–27). Tübingen: Narr.

Byram, M. (1994) Cultural learning and mobility: The educational challenge for foreign language teaching (1). *Fremdsprachen und Hochschule* 41, 5–22.

Corder, S.P. (1981) *Error Analysis and Interlanguage*. Oxford: Oxford University Press.

Doyé, P. (1992) Fremdsprachenunterricht als Beitrag zur tertiären Sozialisation. In D. Buttjes *et al.* (eds) *Neue Brennpunkte des Englischunterrichts*. Frankfurt/M. u.a.: Lang.

Edmondson, W.J. and House, J. (1998) Interkulturelles Lernen: Ein überflüssiger Begriff. *Zeitschrift für Fremdsprachenforschung* 9 (2), 161–188.

Fairclough, N. (1992) Discourse and text: Linguistic and intertextual analysis within discourse analysis. *Discourse and Society* 3, 193–219.

Finkbeiner, C. and Koplin, C. (2001) Fremdverstehensprozesse und interkulturelle Prozesse als Forschungsgegenstand. In A. Müller-Hartmann and M. Schocker-von Ditfurth (eds) *Qualitative Forschung im Bereich Fremdsprachen lehren und lernen* (pp. 114–136). Tübingen: Narr.

Fitch, K.L. and Philipsen G. (1995) Ethnography of speaking. In J. Verschueren *et al.* (eds) *Handbook of Pragmatics* (pp. 269–278). Manuel. Amsterdam: Benjamins.

Foerster, H. von (1996) Lethologie. Eine Theorie des Lernens und Wissens angesichts von Unbestimmtheiten, Unentscheidbarkeiten, Unwißbarkeiten. In K. Müller (ed.) *Konstruktivismus* (pp. 1–23). Lehren – Lernen – Ästhetische Prozesse. Neuwied: Luchterhand.

Garfinkel, H. (1967) *Studies in Ethnomethodology*. Englewood Cliffs: Prentice Hall.

Garfinkel, H. (1972) Studies of the routine grounds of everyday activities. In D. Sudnow (ed.) *Studies in Social Interaction* (pp. 1–30). New York: The Free Press.

Geertz, C. (1987/1991) Dichte Beschreibung. Bemerkungen zu einer deutenden Theorie von Kultur. In C. Geertz (ed.) *Dichte Beschreibung. Beiträge zum Verstehen kultureller Systeme* (pp. 7–43). Frankfurt/Main: Suhrkamp.

Glasersfeld, E. von (1992a) Siegener Gespräche über Radikalen Konstruktivismus. In S.J. Schmidt (ed.) *Der Diskurs des Radikalen Konstruktivismus* (5th edn) (pp. 401–440). Frankfurt/M.: Suhrkamp.

Glasersfeld, E. von (1992b) Aspekte des Konstruktivismus: Vico, Berkeley, Piaget. In G. Rusch and S.J. Schmidt (eds) *Konstruktivismus. Geschichte und Anwendung* (pp. 20–33). Frankfurt/M.: Suhrkamp.

Grau, M. (2001) Forschungsfeld Begegnung. Zum Entstehungsprozess einer qualitativen Fallstudie. In A. Müller-Hartmann and M. Schocker-von Ditfurth (eds) *Qualitative Forschung im Bereich Fremdsprachen lehren und lernen* (pp. 62–83). Tübingen: Narr.

Grotjahn, R. (1997) Strategiewissen und Strategiegebrauch. Das Informationsverarbeitungsparadigma als Metatheorie der L2-Strategieforschung. In U. Rampillon and G. Zimmermann (eds) *Strategien und Techniken beim Erwerb fremder Sprachen* (pp. 33–76). Ismaning: Hueber.

Grotjahn, R. (1999) Thesen zur empirischen Forschungsmethodologie. *Zeitschrift für Fremdsprachenforschung* 10 (1), 133–158.

Gumperz, J. and Hymes, D. (1964) The ethnography of communication. *American Anthropologist* special edition. 66 (6), part II.

Hammersley, M. (1992) *What's Wrong with Ethnography? Methodological Explanations*. London: Routledge.

Hartman, G. (2000) *Das beredte Schweigen der Literatur. Über das Unbehagen an der Kultur*. Frankfurt/M.: Suhrkamp.

Hejl, P.M. (1992) Konstruktion der sozialen Konstruktion: Grundlinien einer konstruktivistischen Sozialtheorie. In S.J. Schmidt (ed.) *Der Diskurs des Radikalen Konstruktivismus* (5th edn) (pp. 303–339). Frankfurt/M.: Suhrkamp.

Hu, A. (1999) Interkulturelles Lernen. Eine Auseinandersetzung mit der Kritik an einem umstrittenen Konzept. *Zeitschrift für Fremdsprachenforschung* 10 (2), 277–303.

Hu, A. (2001) Zwischen Subjektivität und dem Anspruch auf Exploration authentischer Perspektiven: Forschungsmethodische Anmerkungen zu einer interpretativ-ethnografischen Studie. In A. Müller-Hartmann and M. Schocker-von Ditfurth (eds) *Qualitative Forschung im Bereich Fremdsprachen lehren und lernen* (pp. 11–39). Tübingen: Narr.

Hunfeld, H. (1998) *Die Normalität des Fremden. Vierundzwanzig Briefe an eine Sprachlehrerin.* Waldsteinberg: Heidrun Popp.

Hutto, D.D. (2000) *Beyond Physicalism.* Amsterdam/Philadelphia: Benjamins.

Hymes, D. (1979) *Soziolinguistik. Zur Ethnographie der Kommunikation.* Edited by F. Coulmas. Frankfurt/M.: Suhrkamp.

Köpf, G. (ed.) (1981) *Rezeptionspragmatik.* Beiträge zur Praxis des Lesens. München: Fink.

Krüssel, H. (1993) *Konstruktivistische Unterrichtsforschung. Der Beitrag des Wissenschaftlichen Konstruktivismus und der Theorie der persönlichen Konstrukte für die Lehr-Lern-Forschung.* Frankfurt/M. u.a.: Lang.

Lahaie, U. (1995) *Selbstlernkurse für den Fremdsprachenunterricht. Eine kritische Analyse mit besonderer Berücksichtigung von Selbstlernkursen für das Französische.* Tübingen: Narr.

Lamneck, S. (1988) *Qualitative Sozialforschung. Band 1: Methodologie.* München/Weinheim: Beltz.

Maturana, H.R. (1978) *Biology of Language.* German edition (1982) *Erkennen. Die Organisation und Verkörperung von Wirklichkeit. Ausgewählte Arbeiten zur biologischen Epistemologie.* Braunschweig: Wiesbaden.

McLaughlin, B. and Heredia, R. (1996) Information-processing. Approaches to research on second language acquisition and use. In W.C. Ritchie and T.K. Bhatia (eds) *Handbook of Second Language Acquisition* (pp. 213–228). San Diego, CA.: Academic Press.

Müller-Hartmann, A. (2001) Fichtenschonung oder Urwald? Der forschende Blick ins vernetzte fremdsprachliche Klassenzimmer – Wie Triangulation und Interaktionsanalyse der Komplexität gerecht werden können. In A. Müller-Hartmann and M. Schocker-Ditfurth (eds) *Qualitative Forschung im Bereich Fremdsprachen lehren und lernen* (pp. 206–237). Tübingen: Narr.

Müller-Hartmann, A. and Schocker-von Ditfurth, M. (eds) (2001a) *Qualitative Forschung im Bereich Fremdsprachen lehren und lernen.* Tübingen: Narr.

Müller-Hartmann, A. and Schocker-von Ditfurth, M. (2001b) Einleitung. In A. Müller-Hartmann and M. Schocker-von Dithfurth (eds) *Qualitative Forschung im Bereich Fremdsprachen lehren und lernen* (pp. 2–10). Tübingen: Narr.

Mummert, I. (1991) Die Unsterblichkeit der Grille und der Ameise oder,Enfin un amour qui passera l'hiver'. Freies Schreiben mit Fabeln (Sek. I). *Der fremdsprachliche Unterricht – Französisch* 25 (3), 28–32.

Piaget, J. (1972) Sprache und intellektuelle Operationen. In H.G. Furth (Hrsg.) *Intelligenz und Erkennen* (pp. 176–190). Frankfurt/M.: Suhrkamp.

Pishwa, H. (1998) *Kognitive Ökonomie im Zweitsprachenerwerb.* Tübingen: Narr.

Popper, K.R. (1972) *Objective Knowledge.* German edition (1994) *Objektive Erkenntnis. Ein evolutionärer Entwurf* (2nd edn). Hamburg: Hoffmann u. Campe.

Riemer, C. (1997) *Individuelle Unterschiede im Fremdsprachenerwerb. Eine Longitudinalstudie über Wechselwirksamkeit ausgewählter Einflußfaktoren.* Baltmannsweiler: Schneider.

Rusch, G. (2000) Kognitive Autonomie und Lernwirklichkeit: Plädoyer für eine Authentifizierung von Schule und Unterricht. In M. Wendt (ed.) *Konstruktion statt Instruktion. Neue Zugänge zu Sprache und Kultur im Fremdsprachenunterricht* (pp. 73–83). Frankfurt/M. u.a.: Lang.

Schlak, T. (2000) *Adressatenspezifische Grammatikarbeit im Fremdsprachenunterricht. Eine qualitativ-ethnographische Studie.* Baltmannsweiler: Schneider.

Schocker-von Ditfurth, M. (2001) Die Suche nach einem gegenstandsangemessenen Ansatz zur Erforschung von Lernprozessen in komplexen pädagogischen Handlungsfeldern: Grundsätze und Verfahren ethnografischer Forschung. In A. Müller-Hartmann and M. Schocker-von Ditfurth (eds) *Qualitative Forschung im Bereich Fremdsprachen lehren und lernen* (pp. 84–113). Tübingen: Narr.

Schüle, K. (1995) Fremdverstehen im fremdsprachendidaktischen Feld. Einige sozialwissenschaftliche und fremdsprachengeschichtliche Gesichtspunkte. *Neusprachliche Mitteilungen* 48 (2), 78–86.

Schütz, A. and Luckmann, T. (1979) *Strukturen der Lebenswelt* (Vol. 1). Frankfurt/M.: Suhrkamp.

Segermann, K. (1996) Fremdsprachenforschung als Vexierbild: Kritische Anspielungen. *Zeitschrift für Fremdsprachenforschung* 7 (1), 96–105.

Selinker, L. (1992) *Rediscovering Interlanguage*. Harlow/Essex: Longman.

Stangl, W. (1987) *Das neue Paradigma in der Psychologie. Die Psychologie im Diskurs des radikalen Konstruktivismus.* Braunschweig/Wiesbaden: Vieweg.

Strauss, A. and Corbin, J. (1990) German edition (1997) *Basics of Qualitative Research*. Newbury Park: Sage.

Titscher, S., Wodak, R., Meyer, M. and Vetter, E. (1998) *Methoden der Textanalyse*. Leitfaden und Überblick: Opladen: Westdeutscher Verlag.

Wendt, M. (1993) Fremdsprache und Fremdheit. Zu den Aufgaben des Fremdsprachenunterrichts aus der Sicht einer konstruktivistisch orientierten Fremdheitswissenschaft. *Der fremdsprachliche Unterricht – Französisch* 27 (10), 46–47.

Wendt, M. (1996) *Konstruktivistische Fremdsprachendidaktik*. Lerner-und handlungsorientierter Fremdsprachenunterricht aus neuer Sicht. Tübingen: Narr.

Wendt, M. (ed.) (2000a) *Konstruktion statt Instruktion*. Neue Zugänge zu Sprache und Kultur im Fremdsprachenunterricht. Frankfurt/M. u.a.: Lang.

Wendt, M. (2000b) Kognitionstheorie und Fremdsprachendidaktik zwischen Informationsverarbeitung und Wirklichkeitskonstruktion. In M. Wendt (ed.) *Konstruktion statt Instruktion*. Neue Zugänge zu Sprache und Kultur im Fremdsprachenunterricht (pp. 15–39). Frankfurt/M. u.a.: Lang.

Wendt, M. (2002) Empirische Methoden im Spiegel neuerer Qualifikationsschriften zur Fremdsprachenforschung. In H. Küpers and M. Souchon (eds) *Appropriation des langues au centre de la recherche*. Frankfurt/M. u.a.: Lang.

Wodak, R. (1996) *Disorders of Discourse*. London: Longman.

Zeki, S. (1999) *Inner Vision. An Exploration of Art and the Brain*. Oxford: Oxford University Press.

Printed in the United Kingdom by
Lightning Source UK Ltd., Milton Keynes
140265UK00001BA/1/A

194594